Highcastle

STANISLAW LEM

Highcastle

A REMEMBRANCE

Translated from the Polish by Michael Kandel

A HELEN AND KURT WOLFF BOOK

HARCOURT BRACE & COMPANY

New York   San Diego   London

Wydawnictwo Literackie, Krakow 1975

English translation copyright © 1995 Harcourt Brace & Company

Requests for permission to make copies of any
part of the work should be mailed to:
Permissions Department, Harcourt Brace & Company,
6277 Sea Harbor Drive, Orlando, Florida 32887-6777.

This is a translation of Wysoki zamek.

Library of Congress Cataloging-in-Publication Data
Lem, Stanisław.
[Wysoki zamek. English]
Highcastle/by Stanislaw Lem; translated from the Polish by
Michael Kandel.—1st. ed.
p. cm.
ISBN 0-15-140218-3
1. Lem, Stanisław—Childhood and youth.   2. Authors, Polish—20th
century—Biography.   3. L'viv (Ukraine)—Biography.
I. Kandel, Michael.   II. Title.
PG7158.L392A3813   1995
891.8'537—dc20   95-7882
[B]

Designed by Lori J. McThomas
Printed in the United States of America
First U.S. edition

A B C D E

PROLOGUE

Now I see how far I strayed from the goal I set myself when I began this book. I intended to entrust the task to my memory, giving it free rein and following it obediently. Going on the assumption that if the mind preserves, then what it preserves must be worth preserving. Perhaps I hoped that my scattered recollections, like multicolored slivers from a broken kaleidoscope, would eventually arrange themselves into a pattern. Or if not a pattern, then an interconnected multitude of patterns you could order in different ways, albeit primitively and tentatively. And thus I would be not so much recapitulating, in abbreviated form, my childhood—only an abstraction to me now, though my childhood once took up more than a dozen calendars, progressing through all the dates in black and red—not so much recapitulating as drawing, by this method, a portrait of memory itself. Memory, which is not a receptacle altogether independent of me, altogether inanimate, the soul's storeroom with innumerable recesses and cubbyholes, but on the other hand neither is memory I. It is not I because it has autonomy; it is receptive not where I am receptive, indifferent not where I am indifferent—for it often fails to retain what matters to me, while retaining what I care nothing about. And so I wanted to have my memory (and not me) give testimony, and this in turn would reveal what it, my memory, is. I of course take full responsibility for it, though I have no power over it.

This book, then, was to have been an experiment, whose results I would await with curiosity, as if I were not the one speaking, the images and anecdotes issuing instead from the mouth of a stranger. A stranger who, as it happened, sat hidden inside me the way the inner rings of a tree trunk—the days of my childhood and youth—are hidden by the later rings and bark of maturity: the sapling of many decades ago contained within the present tree.

I really don't know when it was that I first experienced the surprise that I existed, surprise accompanied by a touch of fear that I could just as easily have not existed, or been a stick, or a dandelion, or a goat's leg, or a snail. Or even a stone. At times it seems to me that this happened before the war, and therefore in the period dealt with here, but I am not sure. In any case the feeling of surprise was never to leave me, though it did not become an obsession. It was to visit me in different ways, and I would react to it in different ways, sometimes dismissing it as nonsense, a thing to be ashamed of, like a deformity. And the question haunted me: Why are these and not other thoughts entering my head, and what governs and directs them?

For a while I firmly believed that my soul—or, rather, my consciousness—was located four or five centimeters inside my face, behind the nose and a little below the eyes. I have no idea why. This must have been a kind of "prephilosophy," just as once, earlier yet in my life, there was a "pre" to thinking. And that, too, I intended to shake out of the bag of my memory. But it would happen of itself, my task being only to focus on the past as I held the metaphorical bag shaken. This didn't work. Remembering, whether I wanted to or no, I simultaneously imposed an order on what was remembered, an order that clearly pointed in my direction, to the me of today, the so-called man of letters—that is, an adult engaged in one of the least serious and most embarrassing professions: tremendous mental effort given various impressive names that mean nothing, such as "the writer's laboratory." I personally have no such laboratory, or in any case haven't noticed one. But whatever tumbled from my bag of memory, it was instantly given a direction, however subtly. I am not speaking of dishonesty, of alterations made. No, it was spontaneous, unconscious. But I am not making excuses.

It is only now that I see, after the fact, like a detective following the clues of a crime, a crime that employed sleight of hand to tamper even with the evidence that was untouched and did not point in my direction—only now that I see the arrow aimed at me across a quarter of a century. What is even stranger is that I never thought of myself as a "born writer," that it was *hocerat in votis*. I still believe that I was not. In that childhood and the rummage left after it there must have been a great number of intersecting paths, directions to decipher, to discover, most of them confused or broken off or blind alleys. Or perhaps there were no paths at all but only little islands separated from one another in space and time; not a complete chaos, because there was after all a home, school, parents, the fact that when I was very little I stuck a "green wing" to my nose and wore it, and then was bigger, in a school uniform—so there was definitely order. But an order in which you can see, as on an empty chessboard, black-white stripes that go vertically, horizontally, or diagonally. A little effort with the eyes, and you find the structure you want. The chessboard remains a chessboard, and you are not seeing more than what is truly there—alternating black and white squares—yet the perspective, the orientation, can change suddenly.

Something similar, I think, happened with the chessboard of memory opened here. I added nothing, but out of the many possible patterns I favored one. Was this because you automatically look for a theme in a life, an underlying logic? In order not to admit, even to yourself, that so many of your paths were abandoned and so many chances wasted? Or is it simply that you want everything that is and everything that was to make sense, even though it doesn't? As if you couldn't just live your life without analyzing it. In the case of adults, an amorphous, meaningless existence isn't right—but for a child?

I wished to let the child speak, stepping back, not interfering in any way—and instead I exploited him, robbed him, emptied his pockets, notebooks, drawers, to boast to the adults what promise he showed, and how even his little faults were virtues in embryo. I turned my theft into an attractive road sign, practically into a whole highway. And so wrote yet another book—as if I had not known from the beginning, had not guessed, that it could hardly have been otherwise; that all attempts to arrange memories in a strict protocol and without commentary are an illusion. I commented, I interpreted, I spoke too much. And spoke of secrets and toys that were not mine—for I no longer have secrets and toys—and I built a tomb for that young boy and placed him in it, a meticulous, calm, factual tomb, as if I were writing about someone made up, someone who never lived, and who with will and planning could be fashioned according to the rules of aesthetics. It was not playing fair. You do not treat a child that way.

Highcastle

CHAPTER

1

Do you remember the inventory of mysterious things that the Lilliputians found in Gulliver's pockets? Included were a comb that could be used as a picket fence, an enormous pocket watch that emitted a disturbing noise at regular intervals, and many other objects whose use was obscure. I, too, was once a Lilliputian. The way I got to know my father was by climbing all over him as he sat in his high-backed chair. I would rummage through those pockets to which I was allowed access, in his formal black suit that smelled of both tobacco and the hospital.

The left vest pocket contained a metal cylinder that resembled a cartridge used for big-game hunting. This cylinder, when unscrewed, revealed a series of nickel-plated funnels stacked one inside another. These were speculums. In the neighboring pocket I found a pencil worn to a stump. It was set in a golden holder which, when pressed with a force greater than I could muster, gave a click, whereupon more pencil emerged. In the frock-coat pocket was a metal box that opened with a menacing snap and had a velvet lining on which sat a minuscule wallet containing nothing but a patch of suede that unfolded when you unfastened a little button. There was also a tiny silver box with a snap on the lid; inside it was a silver piece attached to the bottom by a flat rubber band, dark violet in color. If you touched it, your fingers would get inky. In the other pocket of my father's frock coat was a round mirror with a hole in the middle, cracked, and having an elastic band and buckle. The mirror made my face huge, turning my eye into a pond where the iris floated like a large brown fish, and my eyelashes were transformed into the surrounding reeds. Across the vest was a gold chain anchored to one side; it held a watch, also golden, with three compartments. The watch had Roman numerals and a small second hand. I wasn't able, no matter how hard I tried, to open the back myself, where little wheels with ruby eyes lived, glittering as they moved.

In this close-up way, I got to know my father. He wore white shirts with thin black stripes, the cuffs fastened to the sleeves by tiny buttons, and a stiff collar attached by studs. I found many of these old collars in our laundry drawers. I enjoyed touching them; their mixture of stiffness and pliability gave me the vague intimation that one could make something interesting and useful out of them. My father's tie was soft in texture and black in color; it looked like a sash and was tied like an ascot. His hat had a soft, wide brim and a rubber band to hold it in place, which rubber band I found perfect for snapping. There were two canes around the house, one of them at times missing; ordinary canes—but my uncle had a truly interesting one, with a silver handle in the shape of a horse's head. And a very old person, hardly able to move, who visited sometimes, used yet another kind of cane, one with an ivory knob. I never got a good look at it, because when he came, I would hide, terrified by his wheezing. I never realized that he wasn't trying to frighten me. He was some uncle or great-uncle but didn't look at all like an uncle to me.

We lived on the second floor of Number Four Brajerska Street. Father and I would take walks to the Jesuit Garden, or up Mickiewicz Avenue toward Saint Jur's Orthodox Church. I don't know why my father took a cane, because he never leaned on it. On winter mornings, when there was too much snow in the Garden, we would stroll up and down Marszalkowska Street, in front of Jan Casimir University, where I craned my neck to stare at the enormous, half-naked stone figures in curious hats that were also stone. Motionless, they performed mysterious duties: one sat, another held an open book propped on a bare knee. Craning my neck constantly was too tiring, so mainly I watched what passed my father at knee level. One time I noticed that he was not wearing his usual shoes with laces, but something entirely different, smooth shoes with no laces. His spats, which he always wore, were gone, too.

Surprised, I asked, "Where did you get those funny shoes?" And a voice came down from above, "What rudeness!" It wasn't my father at all, but a complete stranger, to whom I had attached myself, I don't know how. My father was walking a dozen steps behind. I was terrified. This must have been an unusually unpleasant experience, for me to remember it so well.

The Jesuit Garden was not especially large, and yet I once managed to get lost in it. This happened so long ago, however, and I was so young at the time, that I am not sure whether I remember the event or only heard about it from someone. Between tall shrubs, probably hazel, because they had red branches, there was an enormous barrel filled with water. Thirty years later I used that barrel in a story, "The Garden of Darkness." Yet the Jesuit Garden held no attraction for me, while Stryjski Park did, because it had a little lake in the shape of a figure 8, and on the right there was a path that led to the end of the world. Perhaps because no one ever went there, but I don't know. Or possibly someone told me this, unless I made it up myself and then believed it. Stryjski Park had a complicated topography and was also wonderfully near the exhibition grounds of the Eastern Fair. Winter and summer, the park was dominated by Baczewski Tower, a rectangular structure whose walls were inlaid with colored bottles. I asked if these bottles were filled with real liquor or only colored water, but no one seemed to know.

We usually went to Stryjski Park by droshky, and to the Jesuit Garden on foot, which was a shame, because in front of the university the road was paved with special wooden bricks that under horses' hoofs made a sound as if a great space lay beneath. Not that I didn't enjoy walking to the Jesuit Garden. At the entrance sat a man with a wheel of fortune. Several times I managed to win a cigarette case with yellow ribbons inside to keep the cigarettes in place, but most often I won a two-sided pocket mirror.

There were also ice cream carts, but I was not allowed to eat ice cream. When I got a little bigger, I would sometimes seek out Anusia, a sweet old lady not much taller than I. She wore wire-rimmed glasses and carried a basket of pretzels. The pretzels were either two for five groszy, and those I preferred, the thick ones, a fiver each. For some reason a ten-groszy coin was called a "sixer," and that was a lot of money.

From the Jesuit Garden we went either straight home or by way of Smolka Square, with its statue of Smolka in the center, in order to stop at Orenstein's to buy fruit or a can of cherry compote, which was a rare treat. Always on display in Orenstein's window were pyramids of enticing red apples, oranges, and bananas with oval stickers that said FYFFES. I remember the word but have no idea what it meant. A little farther on, where Jagiellonska Street began, was the Marysienka movie house, which I really disliked, because my mother would take me there when she didn't know what else to do with me. I didn't understand what was happening on the screen and got terribly bored. Sometimes I would slowly slide out of my seat onto the cold floor and on all fours go exploring between people's feet, but that, too, soon grew tiresome. I had to sit and wait for the film to end. The men and women on the screen opened and closed their mouths without voices, while music played. It was a piano at first, then later a gramophone, I think.

But we are going home from the Garden. From Smolka Square you took Podlewski, an uninteresting street, and then two narrow streets, Chopin and Moniuszko, where the strong aroma of roasted coffee told you that our building was next. The iron gate was black and heavy, and then stone steps. I was not supposed to use the back, kitchen stairway, which was spiral and made a tinny, hollow sound when you walked on it. Something drew me to this stairway—perhaps because people said that there were rats in the courtyard you had to cross to get to it. One rat did in fact appear in our kitchen, but I was already ten or eleven then. A frightful thing—when I went after it with a poker, it jumped on my chest. I fled, and don't know what the rat did after that.

We lived in six rooms, yet, with all this space, I didn't have my own. Next to the kitchen was a room that had a bathroom behind a door painted the same color as the wall, an old couch, an ugly cabinet, and under the window ledge a cupboard where Mother stored food. Then there was a hall, the door to the dining room, my father's study, and my parents' bedroom. Special doors led to the off-limits area: the patients' waiting room and my father's office. In our apartment I lived everywhere and belonged nowhere. First I slept with my parents, then on a couch in the dining room. I tried to settle in one place permanently, but somehow it never worked out. When the weather was warm, I would occupy a small concrete balcony off my father's study. From this outpost I would attack the surrounding buildings, because their smoking chimneys turned into enemy warships. I also liked to be Robinson Crusoe, or, rather, myself, on a desert island. As far back as I can remember, I was intensely interested in eating, so my major concern as a castaway was to secure food—paper cones filled with shelled corn or beans, and, when in season, cherries, whose pits also served as ammunition for small arms or simply to squeeze with your fingers. Sometimes I replenished my supplies with coffee grounds or dessert leftovers stolen from the dinner table. I would surround myself with saucers, bags, and cones, and begin the difficult and perilous life of a hermit. A sinner, even a criminal, I had much to brood over and ponder.

I learned how to break into the middle drawer of my mother's dining-room cupboard, where she kept the cakes and pies; I would remove the top drawer and with a knife cut off a thin strip from around the edge of the cake so that no one would notice that it was smaller. Then I gathered and ate the pieces, and carefully licked the knife clean to cover my tracks. Sometimes caution struggled with lust within me for the candied fruit the bakers used to embellish their creations. More than once I could not control myself and robbed the crust of the candied orange, lemon, and melon rinds that squeaked so deliciously between my teeth. Thus I made bald spots impossible to conceal. Afterward, I would await the consequences of my act with a mixture of despair and stoic resignation.

The witnesses to my balcony adventures were two oleanders in large wooden tubs, one white and one pink. I lived with them on terms of neutrality; their presence neither pleased nor bothered me. Inside, there were also plants, distant and stunted relatives of the flora of the south: a rusty palm that kept dying but could not give up the ghost entirely, a philodendron with shiny leaves, and a tiny pine, or maybe it was a fir, which once a year produced clusters of fragrant, young, pale-green needles.

In the bedroom were two things that fed my earliest imaginings: the ceiling and a large iron chest. Lying on my back when I was very small, I would look at the ceiling, at its plaster relief of oak leaves and, between the leaves, bumps of acorns. Drifting into sleep, I thought about these acorns. They occupied an important place in my mental life. I wanted to pick them, but not really, as if I understood, even at that age, that the intensity of a wish is more important than its fulfillment. Something of this infant mysticism passed to real, ordinary acorns; removing their caps seemed to me, for years, a portentous thing, a kind of transformation. My attempt to explain how important this was to me—it is probably in vain.

In the bed in which I slept, my grandparents died. It was Grandfather who left the iron chest, a large, heavy, useless object, a kind of family strongbox from the days before professional safecrackers, when robbers used nothing more sophisticated than a club or a crowbar. The chest, always placed against the door between my parents' bedroom and the waiting room, had flexible handles, a flat lid with flowers carved in it, and in the center a square piece which, when pressed on the side in the right way, popped open to reveal a keyhole. Such cunning today seems touchingly naive, but at the time I thought the black chest was the work of a master craftsman. And I was in complete awe of the key itself, as big as my forearm. I had to wait a long time, impatiently, to grow until the moment when, using both hands and superhuman effort, I was able to turn that key in the lock.

I knew of course that there was no treasure in the chest. What lay at the bottom were a few yellowed newspapers, documents, and a wooden box filled with beautiful thousand-mark notes. I played with this money, and with the cheerful blue hundred-ruble notes, too, which were even more beautiful than the marks, whose brownish color brought to mind dingy wallpaper. There was an incomprehensible story behind the money, something that had suddenly taken away its power. If I had not been allowed to do with the notes as I pleased, I might have thought that some of their power—asserted by ciphers, seals, watermarks, and oval portraits of men in crowns and beards—remained in them and was only slumbering. But since I was allowed to play with them, I had contempt for them, as one has contempt for a splendid thing that turns out to be empty of truth. So I could not rely on the notes for excitement, but only on what might take place inside the black chest when it was long locked—and it was almost always locked, with my silent permission, which of course no one asked me for. Yes, in that darkness inside, something could take place. That was why the opening of the chest was a matter of great weight—literally, too, since the lid was tremendously heavy. From three sides came long bars, and you had to lift them and prop them with a series of special levers; otherwise, I was told, and I believed it, the lid, falling, could chop off a head. Which was what you would expect from such a chest. It was not pretty or pleasant; a gloomy, ungainly thing; yet I long relied on its inner strength. It had a row of holes in its bottom, so the chest could be bolted tight to the floor; an excellent idea. But there were no bolts, none needed now. As time passed, the chest was covered with an old rug and thus reduced to the level of everyday household furniture. Humbled, it no longer counted. On occasion I showed one of my friends the key—it could have been the key to the city gates. But the key got lost somewhere.

Beyond the bedroom was my father's study, which had a big bookcase enclosed in glass, big leather armchairs, and a small round table with curious legs that resembled caryatids, because at the top of each was a little metal head. At the bottom, little bare feet, also metal, stuck out of the wood as if out of a coffin. Which didn't seem at all grotesque to me, too young to make such associations. I proceeded systematically to gouge out all the heads, one after another, and found that they were hollow bronze. When I tried to put them back, they buckled with every movement of the tabletop.

My father's desk, covered with green cloth, stood against the wall by itself and was locked, for it held money: real money. On rare occasions the desk would also store more valuable treasure, more valuable from my point of view then—a box of Lardelli chocolates brought all the way from Warsaw, or a box of candied fruit. My father had to fiddle with a cluster of keys before one of those morsels, rationed out like medicine, would finally appear before me. At which point I was torn between opposite desires: I could either consume the delicacy immediately or prolong the anticipation of its consumption as much as possible. As a rule I ate everything at once.

Also locked in that desk were two objects of great beauty. One was a tiny wind-up bird in a box inlaid with mother-of-pearl, which they said came from the Eastern Fair and had been on exhibit there, a thing not for sale. My father, seeing how the pearl lid opened when you pressed a miniature key, which revealed another lid, one with a golden checkerboard, and how from there jumped a bird smaller than a fingernail, all iridescent and flapping its wings and poking its beak and flashing its eyes, and how it strutted in a circle and sang—seeing this, he set in motion a whole army of stratagems and connections and finally purchased this jewel for an astronomical sum. The bird was taken out and turned on only rarely—so I wouldn't get my hands on it, which would surely have meant the end of the little thing. Although I loved and revered it no less than did my father, I could not control myself. For a while there was another bird that stayed in the desk, one less fine, the size of a sparrow, a wind-up that had no musical ability but only pecked the table vigorously when you put it there. I persuaded my father to let me have it longer, and that was its last hour.

There were little knickknacks, too, in my father's desk. I remember best the eyeglasses no larger than a matchstick, with gold wire frames and ruby lenses, which sat in a gold etui. The less valuable knickknacks were kept in the glass case in the dining room. These were all works of the miniaturizer's art—a table with chessboard and chessmen fixed in place forever, a chicken coop with chickens, a violin (from which I pulled the strings), and assorted pieces of ivory, furniture, and an egg that opened to reveal a group of figures packed together. Also silver fish constructed of tin segments which allowed for movement, and bronze armchairs, each seat the size of a fingertip, upholstered with the softest satin. Somehow—I do not know how—most of these objects survived the years of my childhood presence.

My father's study had old, big armchairs, and the narrow but deep crevices between their cushions and backs slowly gathered a variety of objects—coins, a nail file, a spoon, a comb. I labored mightily, straining my fingers and the chairs' springs, which twanged in pained protest, to retrieve all these, breathing the smell of old leather and glue. Yet it was not such objects that spurred me on but, rather, the vague hope of finding—hatched—objects altogether different and possessing inexplicable qualities. This is why I had to be alone when with quiet fury I set about disturbing those lazy things dark with age. The fact that I found nothing out of the ordinary did not cool my ardor.

But here I should acquaint the reader with the basic principles of the mythology I adhered to then. I believed, not confiding this to anyone, that inanimate objects were no less fallible than people. They, too, could be forgetful. And if you had enough patience, you could catch them by surprise, forcing them to multiply, among other things. Because a penknife kept in a drawer, for example, could forget where it belonged, and you might find it someplace altogether different, between books on a bookshelf, say. The penknife, unable to get back to the drawer in time, would have no choice in such a situation but to duplicate itself, so there would be two of them. I believed that inanimate objects were subject to logic and had to abide by definite rules, and whoever knew those rules could control matter. In an obscure, almost reflexive way I held on to this faith for years—and cannot say I am completely free of it even now.

The library, because it was locked, fascinated me. It contained my father's medical books, anatomical atlases, and, thanks to his absentmindedness, I was able to inform myself in a systematic and thorough way about the differences between the sexes. But, oddly, I was far more impressed by the volumes on osteology. The blood-red or brick-red plates showing men with their skin peeled off like raw steak disgusted me; the skeletons, on the other hand, were so clean. I don't know how old I was when I first thumbed through the heavy black quarto tomes with their yellow drawings of skulls, ribs, pelvises, and shins. In any case I had no fear of those corpses, nor did the study of them give me any squeamish pleasure. It was, instead, like going through a catalog of Erector-set parts, where first we see the individual shafts, levers, and wheels, and then on following pages constructions that can be made from them. It is possible that these osteological atlases appealed to my interest in building things, which did not show itself until later. I thumbed through those books conscientiously, and remember some of the illustrations to this day—the bones of the foot, for example, tied together by ligaments drawn in sky blue, probably for contrast.

Since my father was a laryngologist, most of the thick volumes in his library dealt with diseases of the ears, nose, and throat. These organs and their afflictions I privately considered of little importance, a prejudice I did not realize I had until recently. Prominent in the collection was the monumental dozen-volume German *Handbuch* of otolaryngology. Each volume had no fewer than a thousand glossy pages. There I could look at heads cut open in various ways, innumerable ways, the whole machinery drawn and colored with the utmost precision. I especially loved the pictures of brains, whose different coils were distinguished by every color of the rainbow. Many years later, when in an anatomy lab I saw a real brain for the first time, I was surprised (though of course I knew better) that it was so drab a thing.

Since these anatomical sessions were forbidden, I had to plan them carefully. Such tactical preparation is by no means the privilege only of adults—provided a child is sufficiently motivated. I sat like a rider on the large squeaky leather arm of the armchair, hidden from the door by the doors of the open bookcase, open so I could quickly put the book back in its place. I rested the book against the back of the chair and in that position continued my studying. It is curious, what I thought at the time. I was drawn by the purity and precision of the illustrations. Again, I was to experience disappointment when many years later, as a medical student, I realized that what I had seen in my father's study were only idealizations, abstractions, of the systems of nerves and muscles. Nor can I recall ever feeling that there was any connection between what I saw in the books and my own body. There was nothing disturbing in those plates—perhaps because of their matter-of-factness, the breaking up into parts, and the fanatical completeness, which showed not only anatomical detail but even the fingers and hooks used to part the cut skin for better viewing. There were other books there also, with illustrations indeed frightful, but too frightful for me to fear them either. These showed wounds of the face, in war: faces without noses, without jaws, without earlobes or eyes, and even faces that were without a face, being only a pair of eyes among scars, with an expression that said nothing to me, for I had nothing with which to compare it. I might have shuddered a little, but only as you shudder listening to a fairy tale. In fairy tales, awful things happen, in fact are expected to happen, and the shudder is desirable and pleasant. And many things in those books were funny: artificial limbs, artificial noses attached to eyeglasses, artificial ears on headbands, little masks that smiled, clever plugs to fill holes in cheeks, and false teeth and palates. All this seemed to me a masquerade grown-ups played, a little mystifying, like so many of their games, but containing nothing bad or shameful. There was only one thing, not a book, that made me uneasy. It lay on one of the shelves, in front of the gilded spines of thick tomes: a bone, a temporal bone removed by surgery of the middle ear, by a mastoidectomy. I knew only that it was a bone, similar in weight and touch to the bones sometimes found at the bottom of a bowl of soup. On the shelf, as if set there on purpose, it alarmed me a little. It had a definite smell, mostly of dust and old books, but with a whiff of something else, sweetish, rotten. Sometimes I would take long sniffs of it to figure out what it was, as if smell was the sense that led me. Then at last I would feel a slight revulsion and put the bone back, making sure it lay exactly in the same place.

The lower shelves were filled with stacks of French paperbacks, frayed, torn, and without covers, as well as some magazines—one was called *Uhu* and was in German. The fact that I could read titles doesn't help establish the time of this memory, since I could read from the age of four. I would leaf through the crumbling French novels because they had amusing fin-de-siècle illustrations. The texts must have been spicy, though this is a present-day conclusion, a reconstruction based on memories half-effaced by the passage of time.

On some pages there were ladies in elegant dignified poses, but several pages later the dignity was suddenly replaced by lace underwear, a man escaping through a window and losing his pants while ladies in long black stockings and nothing else were running around the room. I see now that the proximity of these two kinds of books was peculiar, and the way, too, that I leafed through everything, straddling the armchair as I went, without concern or hesitation, from skeletons to erotic nonsense. I accepted, as one accepts the clouds and trees. I was learning about the world, accustoming myself to it, and found nothing dissonant in it.

On the bottom shelf was a metal tube, wider at one end, and in it was a scroll of unusually thick, yellowish paper. Attached to the scroll, a black-and-yellow twisted cord led to a small flat canister that contained something resembling a tiny bright-red pastry with writing in high relief. This was my father's medical diploma, on parchment, beginning with the enormous, lofty words *Summis Auspiciis Imperatoris Ac Regis Francisi Iosephi.* The tiny pastry—into which I gingerly tried to sink my teeth once or twice, but no more, because it didn't taste good—was the grand seal, wax, of the University of Lvov. I knew that the tube contained a diploma because my father told me so, but I had no idea what a diploma was. I was also told not to pull it out of the tube, and that parchment was made from donkey hide, which I didn't believe. Later I was able to read a few words, though not understanding anything. It was only in my first year of gymnasium, I believe, that I could make sense of those lofty words.

This example of the diploma illustrates the process of the repeated updating of our knowledge of objects and phenomena. I went gradually from level to level, each time learning the next version of the thing, and in this there was nothing remarkable. Everyone knows it—everyone first learned the version of the stork and then the more realistic explanation of his own genesis. The point is that all the earlier versions, even those as patently false as the one with the stork, are not discarded completely. Something of them remains in us; they mesh with succeeding versions and somehow continue to exist—but that is not all. As far as the facts are concerned—say, in the case of my father's diploma—it is not difficult to determine what the correct version is, the one that counts. It is otherwise with experience. Each experience has its weight, its authority, which does not admit of argument and depends only on itself. And herein lies the problem, for the sole guardian and guarantor of the authenticity of experience is memory. True, you can say that there are "doubtful" experiences, on the order of my fantasizing about the black iron chest. But it is not always possible to make such a categorical judgment.

To the side in my father's bookcase was a row of tightly packed books which I left alone, having found that they had no pictures. I remember the color and weight of some of them, nothing more. I would give a great deal now to know what my father kept there, what he read, but the library was swallowed whole by the chaos of war, and so much happened afterward that I never asked. And thus the child's version—primitive, false, really no version at all—remains the final one for me, and this applies not only to those books but also to a multitude of things, some of them dramatic, which were played out over my head. Any attempt of mine to reconstruct them, using logic and guesswork, would be a risky enterprise indeed, perhaps a fantasy, moreover a fantasy spun not by a child. So I think I had better not.

The dining room, as I mentioned before, contained, besides the usual set of chairs and a table that opened for larger groups, a very important cupboard, the abode of desserts, with the shelf where Mother kept the "nips," her specialty. Near the window was a fluffy rug on which I loved to sprawl while reading books—now my own books. But because the act of reading was too passive, too simple, I would rest a chair leg on my calf or knee or foot and with little movements keep the chair at the very brink of falling. Sometimes I would have to stop in midsentence to catch the chair to avoid the noise that would call the household's attention to me, which I didn't want. But I'm getting ahead of myself, always a problem in this kind of account.

As far back as I can remember, I was frequently ill. Various quinsies and flus put me in bed, and generally that was a time of great privileges. The whole world revolved around me, and my father asked me in detail how I felt, establishing between us certain passwords and signs which would describe how I felt with incredible precision, to infinitesimal degrees on a scale that didn't exist. I was also the object of complicated procedures, some not exactly pleasant, such as drinking hot milk with butter. But inhaling vapor was great entertainment. First a large washbasin full of hot water was brought in, and Father would add an oily liquid from a bottle with a worn cork. Then he went to the kitchen, where a cast-iron lid was being heated over the flames. He brought it in, red hot, with a pair of tongs and put it in the basin, and my job was to breathe in the aromatic steam. It was a wonderful spectacle, the furiously boiling water, the hissing cherry-red iron, blackened flakes of it falling off, and in addition I got to float things in the basin, whatever was in reach, a toy duck, a wooden pen box. I hope I did not fake pain I did not feel. There must have been the temptation to do this, since my father could not refuse me anything when I was sick. The bird in the mother-of-pearl box sang for me then, and I was allowed to play with the gold eyeglasses with the ruby lenses, and when my father came home from the hospital, he brought "packies" filled with toys. Illness was certainly profitable. Thanks to a sore throat I got a wooden limousine large enough for me to ride sitting astride its roof. There were illnesses, of course, like the stone in my bladder; the pain and fever from that made all gifts and games inadequate compensation. Yet one way or another I always returned to health.

When I was well, I would spend a lot of time by myself. I explored our apartment on all fours, since being a beast increased my sense of smell. So seriously did I take this animal impersonation that I developed thick calluses on my knees, and had them even in the higher grades of elementary school.

It is time now to talk about my nasty side. I ruined all my toys. Possibly my most shameful deed was the destruction of a lovely little music box of shiny wood, in which under a glass lid little golden wheels with spokes turned a brass cylinder that made crystalline music. I was not to enjoy this marvel for long. I got up in the middle of the night, apparently decided, because I didn't hesitate at all, lifted the glass lid, and peed into the works. I couldn't explain later to the alarmed household what had prompted this nihilistic act. A Freudian psychologist, I am sure, would have labeled me with some appropriate terminology. In any case, I grieved over the silencing of that music box no less sincerely than many a rapist-murderer has grieved over his freshly slain victim.

Unfortunately, this was not an isolated incident. I had a little miller who, when you wound him up, would carry a sack of flour up a ladder to a storeroom, descend for another, carry it up, and so on, endlessly, because the sacks thrown in the storeroom meanwhile traveled back down to the foot of the ladder. I had a man in a diving suit inside a jar sealed with rubber, which, when pressed, would send the diver deeper into the water. I had birds that pecked, carousels that turned, racing cars, dolls that did somersaults, and I disemboweled them all, without mercy, pulling wheels and springs out from under the bright paint. For my magic lantern made by Pathé, with the enameled French rooster, I had to use a big hammer, and even so the thick lenses resisted its blows for a long time. A mindless, repulsive demon of destruction lived inside me. I don't know where it came from or what happened to it later.

When I was a little bigger, but only a little bigger, I no longer dared grab instruments of murder and strike—simply, with childhood innocence—because, apparently, I had lost that innocence. Now I looked for various pretexts. For example, that something inside needed fixing, adjusting, examining. A lame story, since I didn't know how to fix anything, nor did I even make an effort. And yet I felt I had a right to do what I did, and when my mother scolded me once for starting to hammer a nail into the dining-room cupboard in order to set up my toy train, I was resentful for a long time. Only Wicus, a trim little sawdust-filled boy doll with reddish blond hair, was exempt from the sphere of total destruction. I made him clothes and shoes, and he hung around in the apartment afterward, probably up to the war itself. Once, in the rush of an irresistible urge, I began to do him in, but immediately stopped and sewed up the hole in his stomach, or perhaps it was a hand pulled off; I don't remember. I had long conversations with him, but we never talked about this.

Having no room of my own, I ranged over all the rooms, and slowly grew wilder. I stuck half-eaten candies under the table, where after years they made veritable geological formations of sugar. From my father's suits pulled out of the closet I built mannequins on sofas and chairs, stuffing their sleeves with rolled paper and filling out the body with whatever lay at hand. When chestnuts were in season, I tried to do something with those beautiful things, which I loved so much I never had enough of them. Even as they spilled from my pockets, I would put more in my underpants. But I found out that chestnuts, deprived of their freedom and kept in a box, quickly lost their wonderful luster and turned dull, wrinkled, ugly. I tore open enough kaleidoscopes to have supplied a whole orphanage, and yet I knew that all they contained was a handful of bits of colored glass.

In the evenings I liked to stand on the balcony and watch the dark street come alive with light. The lamplighter, out of nowhere, silent, appeared, stopped for a moment at each street lamp, raising his rod, and instantly a timid glowworm grew into a blue flame. For a while I wanted to be a lamplighter.

Of the two powers, the two categories that take possession of us when we enter the world (from where?), space is by far the less mysterious. It, too, undergoes transformations, but their nature is simple: all space does is shrink with the passage of years. That is why the dimensions of our apartment slowly dwindled, as did the Jesuit Garden, and the stadium of the Karol Szajnocha II State Gymnasium, where I went for eight years. True, it was easy for me to overlook these changes, because at the same time I was growing more active and independent, venturing into Lvov more and more boldly. The coming together of places familiar to me was hidden by a series of adventures of ever-increasing range. That is why one becomes aware of the reduction only later.

Space is, after all, solid, monolithic; it contains no traps or pitfalls. Time, on the other hand, is a hostile element, truly treacherous, I would even say against human nature. First, I had great difficulty, for years, with such concepts as "tomorrow" and "yesterday." I confess—and I never told this to anyone before—that for a very long time I situated both of them in space. I thought that tomorrow was above the ceiling, as if on the next floor, and that at night, when everyone was sleeping, it came down. I knew of course that on the third floor there was not tomorrow but only a couple who had a grown daughter and a shiny gold box filled with greenish candy that stuck to your fingers. I didn't really like that candy, which filled my mouth with the chill of eucalyptus, but I enjoyed receiving it, because it was kept in a rolltop desk that roared like a waterfall when it was opened. So I understood that by going upstairs I would not catch tomorrow red-handed, and that yesterday was not below us, because the landlord and his family lived there. Even so, I was somehow convinced that tomorrow was above us and yesterday below—a yesterday that did not dissolve into nonexistence but continued, abandoned, somewhere under my feet.

But these are introductory, and elementary, remarks. I remember the gate, stairs, doors, hallways, and rooms of the house on Brajerska Street where I was born, and many people, such as the neighbors mentioned, but without faces, because those faces changed, and my memory, ignorant of the inevitability of such change, was helpless, as a photographic plate is helpless with a moving object. Yes, I can visualize my father, but I can see his figure and clothes more clearly than his features, because images from many years are superimposed and I do not know how I want to see him, the man turned completely gray or the still vigorous fifty-year-old. And it is the same with everyone I knew for a long enough time. When the photographs and portraits are lost, our complete defenselessness against time becomes apparent. You may learn of its action early in life, but that is theoretical knowledge and not useful. When I was five, I knew what old and young meant, because there was old butter and a young radish, and I knew a bit about the days of the week and even about years (the twenties were light in color and then grew dark toward 1929), and yet basically I believed in the immutability of the world. Of people especially. Adults had always been adults, and when they used diminutives with each other, I was slightly shocked—it was inappropriate; diminutives were for children. How absurd that one old man should say to another "Stasiek."

So time was for me then a motionless, paralyzed, passive expanse. A great deal took place in it, as in the sea, but time itself remained stationary. Every hour of school was an Atlantic Ocean one had to cross with manful determination; from bell to bell whole eternities passed, fraught with peril, and the summer vacation between June and September was an eon. I describe this unbelievable duration of hours and days as if I had only heard it from someone else and not experienced it myself, because I can now neither picture it nor conceive it. Later, imperceptibly, everything speeded up, and let no one tell me that impressions lie because all clocks measure the same rhythm of passing. My answer is, it is just the opposite: the clocks lie, because physical time has nothing in common with biological time. Physics aside, how does the time of electrons and cogs concern us? It always seemed to me there was some hidden trickery in the comparison, a vile deceit masked by the computational methods that equated all kinds of change. We come into this world trusting that things are as we see them, that what our senses witness is happening, but later it turns out, somehow, that children grow up and grown-ups start to die.

CHAPTER

2

Norbert Wiener begins his autobiography with the words "I was a child prodigy." What I would have to say is "I was a monster." Possibly that's a slight exaggeration, but as a young boy I certainly terrorized those around me. I would agree to eat only if my father stood on the table and opened and closed an umbrella, or I might allow myself to be fed only under the table. I don't actually remember these things; they are beginnings that lie beyond the boundary of memory. If I was a child prodigy, it could only have been in the eyes of doting aunts. A sensitive child, definitely. Which accounts for my very early affinity for poetry. Even before I was able to read, I recited poems, often before guests. There was one about a mosquito that fell off an oak, but I couldn't finish it, because when I reached the place where the fatal effects of that fall became apparent (the mosquito broke its back), I would start bawling and would have to be led away, sniffling in despair. There were few beings then for whom I felt such fervent, tragic sympathy as for that mosquito. The power of literature over me had revealed itself *in hoc signo*.

In my fourth year I learned to write, but had nothing of great importance to communicate by that means. The first letter I wrote to my father, from Skole, having gone there with my mother, was a terse account of how all by myself I defecated in a country outhouse that had a board with a hole. What I left out of my report was that in addition I threw into that hole all the keys of our host, who also was a physician. But the author of the prank may not have been I—there was a local boy there with me, my age, and it is unclear who had the keys last. Fishing them out was not at all easy.

In those days, of all the sights and monuments Lvov had to offer, Zalewski's Confectionery on Academic Street attracted me most. I must have had good taste, because since that time I have not seen anywhere pastry displays done with such flair. These were actually tableaux in metal frames, changed several times a year, backdrops for mighty statues and allegorical figures made of marzipan. Some great artists, Leonardos of confectionery, realized their visions here, and especially before Christmas and Easter there were marvels cast in almond paste and chocolate.

Sugar Santa Clauses, their sacks overflowing with goodies, pulled on the reins of sleighs, and hams and fish in aspic sat on plates, all made of icing with marzipan inside—and here my information is not secondhand. Even the lemon slices in the aspic were the work of confectionery sculpture. I remember pink pigs with chocolate eyes, and every variety of fruit, mushroom, meat, plant; and there were forests and fields, too, as if Zalewski could reproduce the whole cosmos in sugar and chocolate, using shelled almonds for the sun and icing for the stars. In any case this great master knew how to capture my yearning, anxious, untrusting soul in a different way each season, to conquer me with the eloquence of his marzipan carvings, etchings of white chocolate, Vesuviuses of whipped cream whose volcanic bombs were heavily candied fruit. The cakes cost twenty-five groszy, an awful lot of money considering that a large roll cost five and a lemon about ten, but I suppose you had to pay Zalewski for the panoramas, the sweet, festive battle scenes that rivaled a Raclawicka exhibit.

On Academic Street there was another confectioner, whose creations appealed more to the stomach than the eye. With that store I have less happy associations. My father's older brother, Uncle Fryderyk, once took me for a pleasure ride in a two-horse droshky, I wearing my best clothes and white lace collar, but we ended up at the dentist, who pulled out one of my baby teeth. On the way home, I wailed, my lace spattered with drool and blood, and my uncle tried to appease my indignation at the betrayal by buying me pistachio ice cream at that confectionery. My father, apparently lacking the courage to assist at such terrible scenes, was absent on this occasion.

In Mikolasch's Arcade there was another candy store, which served Italian ice cream. It was here, much later, that my cousin Stefan, a huge hulk of a boy, would challenge me to duels, unfair duels, because we ate ice cream and the one who lost by eating less had to pay for both. Stefan had more room. I remember going home from there, along the glass-covered arcade, walking stiffly, my stomach turned into an iceberg of vanilla.

At the start of Academic Street, not far from the Hotel George, was another store, this one not a candy store yet very important, Klaften's Toy Shop. I know nothing of its windows or interior, because that sacred place took from me all powers of observation; I approached it in a state of sweet fainting, with a pounding heart, feeling what an ordeal awaited my greed that could not make a choice. At Klaften's you could buy voluptuously heavy flat boxes of lead soldiers, little cannons that shot peas, wooden fortresses, tops, popguns, but no pistols that used ammunition—they were forbidden. Once, at the very beginning, I had a horse, a gray rocker. I can't see it now, but the rough feel of its mane and tail, made of real horsehair, remains on the tips of my fingers. I immediately called it Sir, because it was so large and magnificent, and I was good to it: the runners fell off by themselves, gnawed by the tooth of time.

The other images preserved from my pre-gymnasium days are grouped around events fearsome and violent rather than pleasurable. I know where my aunt lived on Jagiellonska Street, because I was attacked there once, in the hallway, by a giant turkey—what it was doing there I have no idea. For a long time I was afraid to enter that hallway, and would run at lightning speed through the darkness between the double wooden gate and the foot of the terribly squeaky steps. The way to my aunt's apartment was also scary— along an annex gallery slanted so badly toward the court- yard that I thought it would fall at any moment. The whole floor of the vestibule slanted, too, like the Tower of Pisa. Behind one door was a drawing room barred to everybody, with a glistening parquet floor and heavy furniture in linen slipcovers. The room was never used, and I imagine that the mere fact of its hermetic existence satisfied my aunt. Young omnivore that I was, I once entered it, taking ad- vantage of my aunt's momentary inattention or absence, and like a pirate made immediately for the black cre- denza, where a pyramid of big marzipan fruit—apples, ba- nanas, pears—beckoned to me from under a glass cover. I lifted the glass and bit into one of those sweet treasures. Somehow I didn't break a tooth, but neither did I leave any mark on the shining surface. The marzipan was as hard as rock; time had given it armor against my gluttony. This was one of my bitterest disappointments.

They tell me that I almost drowned in Lake Zelazna. I was sitting on the shore, and a lady of our acquaintance was playing with me, tugging on a stick—and at one point she pulled too hard. I sank to the bottom like a stone, with- out even time to be frightened. Everything went green, then dark, then someone was holding me upside down and shaking water out of me. The whole experience is shrouded in fog. I think the bathing was separate for men and women, in which case I must have been with my mother, with the women.

I was a witness only in two other dreadful episodes. The

Human Fly came to Lvov, and I think it was in the middle of town, on Legions Street, that he climbed a high building, using only "a little shoelacing hook," as our maid said—and there were indeed such things, hooks to fasten the buttons and loops on women's shoes. They had a metal handle and a round hook. The Human Fly fell, there was a crowd, police, and the next day, on the front page of what was probably the *New Age*, I saw a photograph of him lifted from the pavement. His pale face was covered with lines like the legs of a giant spider. I think he had fractured his skull. I don't know what happened to him after that.

Another time, the coal in our cellar caught fire or began to smolder. We had guests, and a card game was in progress when the doorbell rang and suddenly there was the threatening brass glitter of firemen's helmets in the hall. The whole building had to be evacuated. We stood in the street watching while the firemen flooded the cellar with their cloth hoses. Then we all went to my uncle, who lived nearby. The fire was put out, but the fear of it stayed with me. For a long time after that I had nightmares in which the fire appeared as a white, windswept person banging on the door of the house and looking in the windows. And during the day, when no one was looking at me, I would get down and touch the floor to make sure it was not hot from flames quietly consuming the apartment below.

Of this fear of fire, however, nothing has remained. It is curious that in a child some experiences activate a mechanism of pathological susceptibility while others make absolutely no impression.

One of the first books I read was about a boy who took an elevator that either rebelled or broke, because it went right through the roof of the building and sailed over the city like a balloon. The author intended to entertain, no doubt, but it terrified me, and even twenty-five years later, stepping into an elevator, I would remember this silly story.

Nor do I know where I acquired my fear of insects. My contemporaries loved collecting beetles, but I couldn't touch them. The same with moths. Mice, on the other hand, I had no fear of, and even profited from this. My mother hated them so much that it was I who had to remove the little corpses from the traps, and when no mice were caught, I would show my mother a gray rubber mouse from a distance and thus receive my burial fee all the same.

It is striking that I have little memory of playmates yet had so much feeling for various objects. I cannot recall the face of a single child but remember perfectly my hoop, even the screws that held the wood together, and how I learned to make the rolling hoop return to me. Could this have been because objects submitted to me completely, whereas living beings had a will of their own, a will that went too much against mine? Because everything that surrounded me, whether of metal or wood, became my plunder, my prey. I waited a long time, years, for the death of our gramophone, or at least for it to grow old, but finally my patience ran out and I opened it up. It was not a machine with a big horn, which I saw only in store windows and illustrations; it was made of wood with a resonating box, an internal speaker, and was called, I think, a Pathephone. I loved turning the crank. There were a few "hit" records, one that had nothing but laughter, some popular songs like "Let's Step on the Gas and Go Faster," and arias, but the device for changing the needle, a spring regulator, interested me more than the music. It was the same with the radio. The first radio appeared in our house about 1929. It was a long box with an ebonite face, knobs that had white grooves and pointers, and sockets for earphones. Although there was a large speaker that resembled a fan, one could barely hear the local station on it. This monumental piece of equipment was powered by storage batteries that had to be recharged. I recall that the first program we picked up from Lvov's radio station was Conrad's "Inn of the Two Witches" read by a man with a voice from the grave. Uncle Mundek, the husband of Aunt Hania from Freedom Street, sometimes came to help my father coax from this Swedish box (the trademark was Ericsson) loud whistles, howls, and the meowing of electric cats. Together they built and adjusted an antenna, a wooden cross on which wires were stretched rectangularly. Only rarely were they able to catch, from behind the curtain of static, a screech of music like a signal from another planet, providing pleasure only by virtue of its great rarity. My uncle would make a note of all remarkable instances of reception, from places such as Milan or Berlin, where the most powerful station in Europe was: Königswusterhausen. This apparatus, too, underwent a slow, long decline, going out of date, and the time came for my pliers and hammer. I took it apart and was disappointed: no toothed wheels, no springs, nothing, only some silver-coated tubes, condensers, and a tangle of wires.

My father feared a variety of things—he never allowed an antenna to be put on our roof lest it draw lightning, and in our ovens only wood was burned, because coal gave off fumes that could suffocate you. I may have inherited his disposition but not the specific forms of it. I liked electricity and was always comfortable with it, as early as when I caught pieces of paper with my comb after it was rubbed. As for poison gases, I tried to produce them, to the extent that it was possible. But these manias—electrical, chemical, mechanical—really developed only in my gymnasium years. Before the thirties I was occupied with the trivial, unoriginal things that fill the lives of little boys. First, I went through various machine metamorphoses—I was a ship, a steamboat, an airplane, I worked my pistons, released the steam, went into reverse, and traces of these routines stayed with me almost until graduation. I remember that even as an adolescent in a gymnasium uniform and in love, I was not above suddenly switching gears on the street, or turning the helm alee and dropping anchor.

Such mimicry is probably a normal stage, although it can annoy an observer, who would like children to be simply children and not tiny adults—I have in mind particularly the many eight-year-old mommies pushing little carriages. An expert would say that children are merely preparing, in their play, for the culture they have entered. In the Middle Ages they no doubt played knights, sieges, and crusades.

Also normal is the tendency to explore one's body and its possibilities. Which with me led to a variety of things. For a while I liked hanging myself and collected the necessary rope, though of course I didn't go all the way. And I would torture myself; for example, tie a string around my finger to make it "go to sleep," or tie myself to a doorknob, or hang upside down on a rope ladder (I had one), or press a finger into my eye socket to see double. But I never stuck peas and beans in my nose or ears, well aware of the bad consequences of that—my father was an otolaryngologist, after all. I don't know where I got the idea, but for quite a while I considered the foot, particularly a bare foot, to be the most indecent part of the human body. Once I got into a terrible fight about this with my cousin Mietek, who was two years older (he perished in Warsaw, like Stefan). We were sitting on a windowsill in our apartment, and I had got him to accept my idea, and the issue was who would be the first to show his foot. Since no one was home, we rolled on the floor a long time, locked in combat. I'm sure a Freudian would take pleasure in this confession, but nothing of the foot idea survived, and I did not become in any way a fetishist.

I dwell on these details because somehow they seem to me more interesting than my later memories. With the passage of time, a child becomes more distinctly, more clearly a member of a group—elementary school, gymnasium—and in his behavior conforms to it, or conforms as best he can. His activity therefore grows more derivative and says less, I think, about his innate qualities, the inherited demons in their genotypic suits, than did his first actions, often performed in solitude. Far more interesting, and more worth study, are the first preferences, the first aversions, which seem to come from nowhere; not that which comes later, which is learned and is often mindless imitation. Small children, as we know, have no fear of even the most terrible physical deformities of those near to them; they simply do not notice. It takes a certain amount of time for them to internalize the norms of society. We certainly do not enter the world with any criteria for distinguishing ugliness from beauty. But this is only hazy supposition, for we do not know if it is actually possible to teach a child a hypothetical everyday aesthetics that is "opposite" the ordinary.

But to return to objects. Clothing was an exception; it didn't interest me. Which I conclude from the fact that I remember nothing of what I wore, with the exception of a pair of lederhosen with green suspenders. In front they had a wide fly, a flap with horn buttons, an uncomfortable, dangerous arrangement, because one could simply be unable to open it in time. I remember wishing I had a regular fly and not a flap like the kind little children wore.

I've said nothing yet about the two rooms in our apartment that were important because they were off limits to me: the waiting room and the examination room. The waiting room was furnished with slipcovered armchairs apparently made of ebony, because when an arm broke off once, you could see blue-black wood. There was also an old glass cabinet with "nips," but not good ones, and trays and silver baskets that were gifts from grateful patients, and an imitation Japanese dagger that was coming apart. And there was a Lvov street arab on a wood pedestal, nameless, since he belonged to no child, a large doll with glaring blue eyes, a short coat full of patches, trousers, a striped shirt, and a felt banana in his pocket. I was not allowed to touch this urchin, which was the reason he survived to the war and even through the first years of it, succumbing finally to the collective, methodical attacks of moths. There were always moths on Brajerska Street, and anyone in the house seeing one was required to give chase, clapping furiously, but I, disgusted by the thought of one squashed between my fingers, always clapped to the side.

My father's examination room was forbidden ground, so

of course I explored it scrupulously whenever I had the chance. The wallpaper had a porcelain-tile pattern, and there was a hard narrow couch, and a cabinet filled with medicine and a few books, also a small desk, a heating lamp, a sterilizer, a metal table with instruments, a white chair for the patient, and an adjustable revolving stool for my father. All very spartan, with one exception. In the cabinet was a black box that had small partitions, and carefully placed in these were the things my father, using the large tubes of his Brüning laryngoscope, had removed from the windpipes and esophagi of his patients—quite innocent things in themselves but awesome when you considered where they had been stuck. The exhibit included a denture with four teeth and a little hook, an open safety pin fished from the trachea of a child, various pins, and beans that had begun to sprout, as if they had intended to settle permanently in someone's nose. There were also coins with verdigris, and a large roll of film. When I was older, my father would sometimes tell me the circumstances surrounding the recovery of these trophies, of how he had hunted, his pistol-grip Brüning in his hand, and he showed me his special long hooks, ingenious forceps, probes. Amazing was the story of the man brought to him choking, fainting, and turning blue. The throat speculum showed an open, unobstructed larynx, but then my father noticed an odd glimmer, like glass. It turned out to be a strip of motion-picture film, which the man, a projectionist, had ingested along with a cheese blintz. No one knew how the film got into the cheese, but it lodged in his throat and acted as a valve, closing and choking him whenever he inhaled. The ordinary objects that my father extracted in great numbers from patients, such as fishbones, did not go into the black box. On holidays we could never finish dinner without the violent sound of the bell downstairs, and Father would immediately get into his white coat, put the mirror on his forehead like a huge third eye, and disappear into the examination room.

I envied him his triumphs, whose sporting rather than medical nature appealed to me, and in great secrecy I would take out the whole Brüning apparatus, connect the long nickel-plated tubes, insert the tiny lightbulbs, and bravely attempt to retrieve from the hose of the vacuum cleaner the foreign bodies I had put there. I would spin on my father's stool until I was dizzy. I would turn on the large thermal lamp, which once supposedly set a woman patient's hair on fire because she had a celluloid clasp or comb in it, but that was before my time. And when I could think of nothing better to do, I would fill the half-liter syringe my father used to flush out ear wax and squirt water through the open window facing the courtyard, now up at the floor above, now down on the landlord's balcony.

As I said before, I learned to read and write early. For my father and mother I made beautiful honorary scrolls decorated abundantly with drawings of flowers. My first reading matter was typical, the usual assortment of fairy tales and poems, such as that one about the mosquito. After the war I came across a collection of children's poems and recognized some that I had read more than thirty years before, and was surprised at what I had found in them as a six-year-old boy. Improbable, inexpressible dramas, and emotions that no longer went together in me now; amazement, terror, but humor, too, lay in wait for me then in the course of the most innocuous words. Why should a story about a spot on the floor that a broom could not sweep clean be full of such gloom, even menace? Why did counting crows without tails become a magic incantation, the perilous summoning of hidden powers or demons? What is even stranger, I told no one about my emotions, fears, forebodings. But probably I could not have expressed or named those states. And perhaps, too, I thought—assuming I was able to think at all about this—that my reaction to reading was the only one possible and therefore perfectly normal. In any case I was a far more sensitive instrument then than I am now; not much stimulus was needed to raise in my head whole edifices of feeling and experience. The authors of children's books truly do not know what they do, do not know with what inflammable material they juggle. They may think they are merely telling an instructive tale, but in the mind of a child it becomes a mystery or a tangled tragedy. Trying to amuse, they teach occult truths; rhyming simply, they lead a seven-year-old mind to catharsis. This beginning, my first reading, was extraordinary. Later, more typically and quietly, I immersed myself in books.

I was Mowgli, of course, and Winnetou, and Captain Nemo. The oddest passages have stuck in my memory for no apparent reason. After the war I bought a copy of Uminski's *Voyage Without Money* and searched page by page for one of its most beautiful lines: "The bullet, having flown with characteristic thunder." It had to do with hunting a crocodile or rhinoceros, but unfortunately this was a revised edition, and that wonderful bullet with its thunder had been taken out, to my great disappointment. And

Valley Without an Exit? Awful things transpired in me when I read it as a boy. Not to mention *Call of the Wild*. Such reading did not permit casual lounging on the window ledge or balancing a chair with my feet or kneeling at the table with my elbows on the tabletop. I had to be very close to completely safe adults, and even then it was sometimes horrible. I didn't like Dickens; he was like a rainy, hopeless autumn. In Dumas, however, I plunged and was lost. It began innocently, with *The Three Musketeers*, and then after a while it seemed that there was not time enough in a life to read all his books.

Later, at the gymnasium, I read everything I could get my hands on, Fredro and May, Sienkiewicz and Verne, H. G. Wells and Slowacki and Pitigrilli. A real stew.

As I read, I usually ate something. I believe I've already made it clear that I was a glutton. But amorous, too. I should mention here my first women. It went in a curious zigzag. Mila first, our laundress. I was probably about five and wanted to marry right away. The poor woman suffered from varicose veins. There were no washing machines in those days, and laundering turned the house into a kind of stifling hell, at least the kitchen and adjoining rooms. An enormous tub was put in the center, the boilers gurgled like a volcano, then the wooden ringer appeared and made an awful racket. I stood in the middle of all this, not bothered by the chaos.

Next I fell in love with my elementary-school teacher. I don't know what she looked like, but I remember that one day she knocked the classmate sitting next to me off his chair. In school you usually got nothing more than a rap of a ruler on your open palm, but this boy was hard, cold, insubordinate, and arrogant, and my beloved spanked him until a cloud of dust rose from his pants. He said not a word and didn't cry, which impressed me enormously.

Gradually my specialty became unrequited love. I fell madly in love with a girl some four years older than I and therefore practically an adult, since I was ten. Transfixed, I watched her from afar in the Jesuit Garden. I was quite fat by that time, my body beginning to assume the shape of a pear, wider below the middle. In the gymnasium I would be even more a pear. I had a pudgy face with eyes that bulged, because I was curious by nature, and my mouth hung open—apparently I thought that that was attractive. I didn't have much chance of success then; however, I had no fulfillment in mind, no idea of what to do with girls other than chase them in the evening, in the Garden, from bush to bush, and frighten them with a flashlight. My love for the girl in the Jesuit Garden therefore had no action, no development, and yet it was unusually intense. I must even have told my parents about it; otherwise I would not have been allowed to spend so much time at my observation post. She probably knew nothing about me; I did not exchange a single word with her. Yet her profile, her chin, her lips are so distinct in my memory, I can see them today.

It is curious that these platonic passions did not interfere with dalliances (if they were dalliances) of a more earthy nature. I could not have been more than eight when my father, entering the kitchen, found me pinching a servant's behind. Embarrassed, he said something like, "Ah, yes" or "Ah, excuse me," and quickly left. It is also curious that I can recall some of my actions from those years, and even feelings, but no thoughts. Possibly my thoughts never went beyond the circle of immediate data, of physical experience.

On Slowacki Street, across from the Central Post Office, was the Cunard Line office, and in each of its windows was a model of an ocean liner. Those magnificent ships accompanied me, filled my dreams; they had everything, brass screws in the steering wheels, rigging, masts, endless portholes in a row, decks, bridges, miniature lifeboats, ladders, and life preservers. I thought about them with hopeless hunger, much as Jack the Ripper must have thought about the women who did not fall into his clutches. His fantasies were surely as bloodless as mine as I stood at the Cunard Line windows, for it was only the acting upon them that led to crime. So it was probably a good thing that none of those two-meter marvels ever came within arm's reach of me, because sooner or later I would have reached for a hammer.

THE CHILD I was interests me and at the same time alarms me. True, I murdered only dolls and gramophones, but you should remember that I was physically weak and feared the reprisal of adults. My father never hit me, my mother sometimes slapped, that was all, but there were many other, less direct, means and methods, from verbal reprimand to withholding of dessert. If four-year-olds equaled their parents in strength, the world would be a different place. They are truly a separate species, and no less complex than adults—but the complexity lies in a different place. For wasn't it with despair in my heart that I demolished my toys? Didn't I regret afterward their loss (independently of the punishments imposed)? And why, if I was so timid, did I relish dangerous situations? Something drove me to lean as far as I could out of the window, even though I knew from the example of the Human Fly what a fall from the third floor could do. I remember how I frightened my uncle one winter vacation in the town of Tatarow when I crawled under a locomotive just as it was about to move, to break off an icicle hanging from a driving rod. I was full of fear that the train would move and cut off my legs, but evidently I desperately needed to get hold of that icicle. Could this have been what psychologists call compulsive behavior, a kind of obsession? I indeed went through periods of counting windows and doors, phases of complicated rituals; I avoided the cracks in the sidewalk when I walked, and with breathing I had awful problems. I tried to hold my breath as long as possible, or to breathe in a special way, not only inhaling but also interhaling, particularly before sleep, and I would put the little pillow and the big pillow under my head just so, build a tent out of the blanket, and so on.

Sometimes, when I was sick, but also when I was perfectly healthy, I would have strange sensations called, as I learned thirty years later, disturbances of the body-image. I lay in bed with my hands on my chest, and suddenly they would start growing, while under their incredible mass I became smaller and smaller. This happened several times, and definitely when I was awake. My hands grew to mountainous size, the fingers turning into enormous closed arches in their monstrous elephantiasis. I was frightened, but only a little, it was so strange—and told no one.

CHAPTER

3

I SEE NOW that I was a lonely child, but was unaware of it then. I wanted a little brother or sister, but I'm afraid what I really wanted was a little slave. I liked to read the advertisements in the paper in which parents put their children up for adoption. Such advertisements were common. If we could take in such a child, I thought, that would be wonderful. The generality of this wish seems to me today a little suspect. Other children didn't visit me very often. Not that it never happened, but it was the exception rather than the rule.

On Sundays in summer and fall, we usually took a ride outside town—always to the same place, Mr. Rucki's garden restaurant located on the road to my uncle's house, near the tollbooth. Paying the toll was an interesting, entertaining break in the trip. I sat with the droshky driver, of course. His name was Kramer or Kremer, but I called him Fatty, and that stuck. He was thickset, had a red face, and was very patient with me. It was from him that I learned the basic things about horses, such as the fact that the horse respects and obeys man because its large eyes magnify everything, so man appears much larger than the horse itself. This is the reason horses are skittish—they think everything is huge! During the long hours while my father, Uncle Fritz, and the rest of the company sat under the fruit trees playing cards, I had to find something to do. Rucki's restaurant had a bowling alley, but for years I lacked the strength to throw the big wooden ball. Sometimes I was able not only to get into a theoretical discussion with Fatty but also to persuade him to unhitch the horse so I could ride it a little. When he refused, it was always politely. Or he slept in the droshky, his feet propped on the driver's seat, and I crawled into the raspberry bushes, where there were lots of cruel thorns. As a last resort, I would sneak up on the cardplayers. My uncle had a derby that intrigued me because it was so hard. I tried with all my might to break its crown, but it resisted, as if a steel plate were hidden under the black felt.

I must have managed to amuse myself, because I don't remember being bored. I had everything, after all—toys, books, modeling clay with which I made elephants, horses (they always came out worst), different kinds of sausage, and dolls. I would take clay out of the doll's belly and insert little intestines, livers, lungs, also made of clay, because by now I knew something about how things inside looked. I liked multicolored clay best, because then you could take the belly of the patient and roll it between your hands until you had a lump with all different layers of color mixed and spread, and from this "dough" you could make the next victim, and so on without end.

Before my gymnasium days I was not that independent, and apart from my immediate neighborhood didn't know Lvov well. I knew a little of Kazimierz Street and the area near Saint Brigid's Prison, a grim building with thick walls, because it was not far from Bernstein Street, where Uncle Fritz had a law office. And Grodecka Street, which we took when we went to the train station, magnificent and vast at the end of Foch Boulevard.

Uncle Fritz lived on Kosciuszko Street, not that far from Brajerska, and I could have gone there myself, though I never did. I was afraid of his apartment at first, because of the bear rug in the middle of the living room, with its open mouth and teeth. It was a long time before I dared put my fingers between those jaws. I loved Uncle Fritz, although he played a cruel joke on me once. He brought me a gift in an enormous package, and I threw myself on it to tear away the wrapping, but this took forever, maybe a quarter of an hour, until, covered with sweat and trembling, I stood surrounded by paper, and in my hand a doll smaller than a bean. My uncle roared with laughter; I was deeply hurt.

If I agreed to go to Kosciuszko Street at all, it was because of the big black piano which nobody ever played. I loved the opportunity to assault the keyboard, making thunderous cacophonies. I had no ear, and thank God my parents did not attempt to inculcate musical ability in me by lessons on an instrument. Besides the numerous heavy, long door curtains of which my uncle's second wife, Aunt Niunia, was so fond, there was fancy furniture on Kosciuszko Street—no doubt imitation Louis this or that. I remember a mirror in a gilt frame (on lion's legs?); a griffin on a stand, of painted wood and with a little African on its back; a chandelier of a thousand pieces of rainbow glass; and a copper pot in a windowless niche—the most interesting thing of all, since it served no purpose.

Uncle Fritz generously allowed me to take home volumes of the old Brockhaus and Meyer encyclopedia, which was piled high in his office. I couldn't manage more than one at a time, they were so heavy. Nor could I read them, not knowing German; but they were full of tables, illustrations, woodcuts. I spent a lot of time over those thick, dusty tomes. The world depicted in them was, in the 1920s, already fossilized, an anachronism, but that didn't bother me. The trains of the 1880s, the iron bridges with garland grillwork, the locomotives with crowned smokestacks, and the passengers, the bearded gentlemen—all that seemed wonderful to me, inexpressibly enchanting. And those ancient dynamos, and devices with wheels that had carved spokes, and the electric motors, and all kinds of latest inventions such as horseless carriages powered by battery (these in the last, supplementary, volume). What amused me was that the books, containing everything, put everything side by side: elephants, birds, plants, reconstructions of mammoths, colorful tables of Prussian medals, portraits of rulers, African physiognomies, vases, gems. I sank deliciously into the encyclopedia, turning each successive volume page by page so as not to miss anything. I don't recall if I had any idea what kind of book this was and what function it served. That probably didn't matter to me. But even if I failed to understand that this was the cataloging and description of an entire world, or, rather, a cross section of one made in the 1880s, I did at least grasp one principle: Everything was equally good, though of course not equally interesting. And this was the perfect complement to the explorations I had carried out in my father's library. More than one engraving inspired me later, when the passion for inventing things fell upon me. In addition, the encyclopedia, when it gained the right of permanent residence in our apartment and was put on the old white shelf in the room by the kitchen, served as a hiding place. Behind certain volumes there was room enough for me to conceal tiny flasks of secret mixtures—or simply of different alcohols that I took discreetly from the bottles in the living-room cupboard.

IT IS SO much easier for me to talk about the objects of my early childhood than about the people. But, then, only the objects—if you can say this—were honest with me, were completely open, hiding nothing: those that were at my mercy and I destroyed, as well as those that I had no power over. Certainly parents and relatives had reasons not to confide in a child. That's only natural. Even so, their problems and affairs did reach me sometimes, in a fragmented, incomplete, unclear way, or else only in long retrospect. I learned more than one thing after the fact, and could fill out this narrative with explanations and glosses which would put things in true perspective—that is, the perspective of an adult—and bring order to an account whose limited point of view must leave many gaps. But this is exactly what I do not wish to do, to create such a double perspective, for I am not writing a history either of my family or of its individual members. My goal is a much more modest one: I am concerned only with the child I was. A child, after all, does not consider his world incomplete, full of gaps, requiring commentary from the vantage point of a hazy future. A child acts instinctively, not by choice, for he is not aware that he constitutes an exception in the world of adult situations. One who describes a society that practices magic should not say at every step that its belief is wrong, should not criticize, speak of madness, advocate rationality as opposed to superstition, and constantly deny the validity of charms and the efficacy of spells. If the spells have no real effect on the material world, they certainly have an effect—a major, decisive effect—on those who believe in them. The same is true with a child. What counts for him is what he experiences and not the correct interpretation of facts; and the sifting of those facts is not a matter of true version versus false but done passively, at the silent command of memory, which registers what it registers—without any possibility of appeal.

CHAPTER

4

Writing about one's childhood is a risky activity, especially for someone like me, who has a terrible memory. Moreover I must keep a tight rein on my professionalism as a fantast, that is, the ability to group details into coherent wholes. With several science-fiction books and one contemporary novel behind me, I have put together biographies of fictitious persons so many times that the addressing now of my own person, and my own person of years ago, should be done only with the utmost self-control. The literary reflex is to build patterns, to order a sequence of events so that it achieves closure in some way, closure and meaning. But I believe this reflex is also a general, fundamental impulse in human nature—manifesting itself in both the individual and the collective. And from the earliest times. For what are myths if not the imposing of order on phenomena that do not possess order in themselves? And all myths, however they differ from philosophical systems and scientific theories, share this with them, that they negate the principle of randomness in the world. Even if chaos itself does not exist in the material world in a pure form, unadulterated by any kind of order, we still will not accept whatever order that can be objectively discerned. Neither a novelist nor a biographer will settle for a statistical explanation, the law of large numbers, the Brownian motion of molecules. Where you have statistical order, which describes the course of events only in a general way, leaving plenty of margin to the operation of blind chance, an author—and not always consciously—will insert order to a degree not found in the real world, an excess of order that may come from wishful thinking, or from limited vision, or from obedience to a reigning methodology or aesthetic. The effect is usually that the represented reality is ennobled. And so we have the idyll of childhood, its sweet innocence—or, if the author wishes to counter that formula, he creates a world of children as little monsters, which is but another kind of biographical formula. To say "everything," disregarding all method, is impossible, because there is always selection and all that changes are the criteria for selection. Anyway, if I rely on memory, I am trusting *it* as the selector, submitting to that which I am able to recall. I therefore believe that the limit of one's ability to remember is the barrier of one's honesty, a barrier that cannot be crossed.

It is unsettling how often I have had the impression, while writing these pages, that I am not presenting events but, rather, a kind of literary travesty of them. Indeed, in *Time Not Lost* I began with my childhood, but after re-writing and reworking that part of the book many times, I finally threw it out completely. It contained a great deal of material taken from early memories, fragments of which were also scattered among other books of mine. Thus I find myself in the awkward position of one who cannot simply reach into a bag of facts, however chaotically they are mixed together, but instead must pull them, as if by force, out of constructs where they have assumed the appearance of truth. One might see this as an ironic variant of the sorcerer's apprentice, or simply of the liar caught in his own lies.

This obviously applies more to accounts of feelings and psychological reactions than to purely physical experience. But it applies to both. Saying which, I undermine—I realize it—the whole idea of separating the interpretation of the experience from the experience itself, as if by separating to purify the latter. But that is impossible; it is like demanding that the truth and only the truth be written. The child I was thus becomes a Kantian *Ding an sich:* I can track it, guess at it, but I will never know to what degree I have succeeded. Never know when my reconstruction goes too far and I am building, from fragments and guesses, a reality that doesn't exist at all.

It is interesting that people in fields far, far removed from attempts to return to "the land of childhood" face similar difficulties. For it turns out that when we desire accuracy and precision beyond a certain point, the objective facts can no longer be separated from their interpretation, since interpretation lies at the very foundation of language—words, grammar, syntax. Interpretation lies there and not perfectly faithful photographs of objects or psychological phenomena. Not a comforting statement, but at least it may absolve. Too much knowledge often is a burden that interferes with action, because one who knows how very many "theories of the child" exist in psychology and anthropology must be aware that no matter how hard he tries to be simple, candid, authentic, he will drift despite himself toward one of those theories, carried by his intellectual and personal predilections, for he sees the child he was through the glasses placed upon his nose by all the years that followed, and there is no help for this.

So much for the child as unknowable being. As the years pass, he becomes more knowable, but at the same time, it seems to me, he undergoes banalization, normalization; that is, he conforms increasingly to the group in which and with which he grows. The eternal dispute of which in a human being are inherited factors and which are acquired through environmental influences now rages only with regard to the first years of childhood. And here breakthroughs may come, in theoretical knowledge and in education—if, for example, it turns out that the learning process and culturization can begin much earlier. Then we could turn toddlers of two or three into individuals capable of doing higher mathematics.

But let us not talk of the future; our subject is the past. For which I can rely upon nothing but my memory. In vain did I try to fill gaps by consulting old books and albums. To be sure, images of streets, squares, and churches seemed familiar, but probably only in the way the nooks and corners of a house are more familiar to the mice than to its legal residents. Strangely enough, it was a map of the city that spoke to me the most, a dry outline, an abstraction of the streets. Apparently the mechanisms of memory, which continue to defy the deciphering of science, are multiform and many-layered. The road from home to the gymnasium—I could walk it even today with my eyes closed, because constant repetition over the years fixed it in my mind, turned it into a "kinesthetic melody," as a psychologist might say. But as a Lvov student I was no more appreciative of the beauty of my surroundings than the mouse is of its. Undoubtedly I passed monuments of architecture, the Armenian Cathedral, the old buildings of Market Square, including the famous Black House, but I remember nothing of that. At seven-thirty in the morning I would add water to my coffee to cool it, then I took Moniuszko Street, Chopin Street, Smolka Square with the stone Smolka in the middle, Jagiellonska Street, and passed the Marysienka Cinema before Legions Street. On the left loomed the cinema, but what drew me, as a lighthouse draws a sailor, was a little building, far less imposing, on the corner of the Square of the Spirit—a kiosk selling Mr. Kawuras's products.

He made halvah, and it came in two different packages, one for ten groszy and one for twenty. I usually got a weekly allowance of fifty groszy, and so on Mondays could wallow in halvah, but from Wednesday on there was gloom. Also I was tormented by a problem of both solid geometry and algebra: Which was better, one package for twenty groszy or two for ten each? The fiendish Mr. Kawuras complicated the solution by giving the packages irregular shapes, and I was never completely sure of the right answer.

Next on the way was Market Square, with the enormous boxlike Municipal Building, the tower of City Hall, the Neptune Fountain with stone lions crouching at the gate, then I went down narrow Ruska to Rampart, where the two-story gymnasium stood, surrounded by trees.

When I did not have a grosz to my name, I would go instead past the Viennese Coffee Shop, so that the sight of those rich walls of halvah behind the glass of the kiosk would not wound my heart. At the coffee shop was the first clock to tell me how much time I had; the next was high on the City Hall tower. They told me if I could still look in some shop window or had to run. And that is really all the eye remembers and almost all that occupied my soul. I was truly like a mouse, and society did what it could, through its educational system, to turn me into a human being. Did I resist? Not much as an individual—more as a member of the student body.

On this subject the most outstanding writers of the world have said things that cannot be surpassed. They have shown school as a complex game, a battle of opposing interests, where the teacher, representing authority and power, attempts to pack the maximum information into the students' heads, while the students, by nature the weaker side, do their best to avoid that information. In this they are not completely successful—but the mindless, desperately stubborn resistance of the class, a mixture of villainy and inertia, does what it can to pervert, besmirch, and discredit everything that implements the learning process. The educational battlefield is not rich in epic scenes, but there are examination duels, mass executions in the form of tests, and all manner of feints, attacks, ruses, and escapes, where every desk becomes a barricade, a piece of chalk can be a missile, and the lavatory is often the only refuge.

Thus arises, from antlike labor hidden in all the cracks and crevices of the official culture, a gymnasium subculture—because the class, maltreating desks and carving graffiti on bathroom walls and drowning flies in inkwells and wetting the chalk and tearing the erasers and drawing mustaches on national heroines and breasts on national heroes, may seem simply to be answering order with chaos, but in reality it is building an order, an order that neutralizes, by the smearing on of nonsense, all the material instruments of instruction. That is why pens are turned into play swords and notebook pages into paper airplanes. There is method to this wild, noisy-horde student madness, as the class seats, entrenched, face the teacher's desk.

I entered the old gymnasium in 1932, and my collar, hook-fastened, had one silver stripe. Each year a stripe was added, and in the fifth year the silver was replaced by gold. But in my second year they changed this system, and I was back to one stripe. Stiff caps with yellow velvet piping (we were called canaries) replaced the soft-visored caps, and the uniforms now were navy blue. The trousers had a light-blue stripe (the lower classes), and the shirts were open at the collar, civilian style. We were also given badges—Gymnasium 2 became Gymnasium 560. The badges started a battle. Each morning before eight, the director and one of the masters would walk about the building, among students doffing their caps to them. Now and then the director would call a student over to see if his badge was sewn in accordance with regulations or only disreputably pinned. Therefore more than one student carried a sewing kit in his pocket, so that, when warned by friends, he could duck into a gateway on Ruska Street and quickly cover the traces of his crime. As for me, my badge was firmly sewn on by my mother, to my chagrin—and I fought this in a round-about way, finally hitting upon what I could do with the badge, in keeping with the above-mentioned subculture. But of that later.

With the old gymnasium went the pewlike benches and desks. They were replaced in almost all the classes by modern desk-chairs with drawers. School benches for me are archaic, a relic of a vanished era. I encountered them only briefly, when they were on their way out, and I cannot think of them without sadness. But, emotions aside, it seems to me that those left should be collected and put in museums alongside relics of Aurignacian and Mousterian cultures. Paleolithic man carved stone; Gymnasium man carved his desk-bench. It was an excellent medium. The carpenters who designed it must have been full of wisdom, foreseeing generation upon generation of students, each new wave attempting to break those wooden chains. With time the edges grew as smooth as ivory, gripped desperately by the hands of countless students called upon by the teacher. Sweat and ink seeped into the thick planks, so that gradually they assumed an indescribable gray-blue-dun color. Nibs of pens, penknives, fingernails, and probably teeth, too, left secret marks, rows of hieroglyphics, layer upon layer, for each generation deepened the work of the one before, and thus craters came into being, and hollows where once there had been knots, made incomparably smooth by Sisyphean labor during endless hours of lecturing. And that is not all. When discipline grew most stringent, and one had to sit with hands folded, the eyes, those servants of the soul, over which the pedagogical body had no power, sought escape by resting on the patterns in the wood. With a little concentration one could silence the teacher's words. As Hamlet bounded in a nutshell could count himself a king of infinite space, so could each student merge with the abstract meanderings on the desk before him, sink into sweet torpor, and escape. True, you could carve things also on a polished desk-chair, but it was not the same. That was done without conviction, without artistry, out of habit only. The old desk-bench had two shallow holes for inkwells, which were a special kind, glass containers with a deep funneled opening designed so the ink would not come out if they were overturned. The ink came out, I assure you, and if it didn't at first, it was helped. Ballpoint pens did not exist and fountain pens were looked down on; we wrote with pen points, which could also be thrown or used to jab one's neighbor. Thereby demonstrating that there is no implement that cannot be put in the service of a goal opposite the one intended by its creator. A culture is passed from generation to generation, so it was known for ages what benches are for—but with these new desk-chairs *obstupuunt omnes* at first. We were not stymied for long, however, and the chairs began losing their legs. This is called vandalism, and vandalism it was, yet not so different really from what monastic scribes in medieval cloisters did when they scratched valuable writing off a parchment to substitute their own uninteresting text.

What Heaven is to a Christian, Highcastle was to each of us. We went there when a class was canceled because the teacher was suddenly indisposed—one of those blissful surprises that fate on rare occasions brings. Highcastle was not a place for truants, too dangerous for that; in the lanes and between the park benches and trees one might meet a schoolmaster. The deserters instead took to the ravines of the Kaiserwald, beyond Sand Mountain, where they sat safely in the bushes and smoked fancy Silesian cigarettes. But in Highcastle we walked openly, making plenty of noise, in the sweet aura of legal idleness, drunk with our sudden freedom. Only two tram stops separated the gymnasium from this delightful place, but we never took the tram; it was too expensive. We usually went up Teatynska Street, and a few dozen steps beyond the place where the rails ended there was a steep drop, and the whole city lay before us, with Sand Mountain on the right, and on the left the park greenery, obscuring the Memorial Mound of the Lublin Union. Far below was the dark tangle of tracks of the Podzamcze train station, with tiny locomotives, and beyond that an airy expanse, light blue and hazy to a green horizon.

In Highcastle there stood a broken wall, a ruin, but I hardly remember it. Thirty years had to pass before I thought about this and learned that Highcastle had been a magnificent building, given its name because there was a Lowcastle in the city. But ruins and venerable monuments were of no interest to me then. What did we do there?

Nothing to speak of. A few times a year my father would take me to the Union Mound or to Sand Mountain, but never during school hours. It was then, during the school day, that possibilities suddenly opened. In my eight years at the gymnasium I must have gone there countless times, but I remember nothing of the place except the low hedges, behind them the sky-blue panorama of the city, and the shade of great chestnut trees. Because it was not really a place, it was a state, so intensely perfect that it could be compared only with the first day of summer vacation—a day not yet touched, not yet begun, when the heart faints with deliciousness because everything is still ahead, but you also feel the urge to loaf, with time spread out like an ocean through all of July and August. At Highcastle, however, we had only one hour, so every minute had to be savored, filled conscientiously with indolence. We dove in, we wallowed, we let ourselves drift, as in a warm river under a sky with white clouds. It was not a Christian heaven full of modest prayer, but a nirvana—no temptations or desires, but blessedness that existed independently. Even our throats, hoarse from howling during recess, were affected by this gust from another world; we screamed a little, yes, but more out of habit than conviction.

We also went there, particularly into the hills behind Sand Mountain, on nature field trips, but that was something altogether different, at least for me, who never liked plants. Our nature teacher, Mr. Noskiewicz, was amazed that even with Rostafinski's classification guide in my hand I could turn grasses and thistles into rhododendrons. Angiosperms, gymnosperms—the names themselves disgusted me; I don't know why. Somehow plants made me nervous.

True, they are in a sense related to us, yet they are satisfied with everything or—what is worse—they are indifferent. With mice, lions, and ants we share a multitude of troubles, we fear, we desire, we strive; but the vegetable kingdom's quiet acceptance of fate seems to me a betrayal of the common cause. Did I hold such eccentric views in my twelfth year? Hardly, and yet my dislike for my green cousins—which has nothing to do with being forced to eat spinach—goes as far back as I can remember.

Returning to the gymnasium from such an excursion, you noticed how small the playing field was, an area cut into the slope of the ramparts and stamped flat by countless feet. It was marked off only with low stone posts connected by an iron rail—no obstacle, but one was forbidden to go beyond that border. We had to stay in the enclosed space, and so used every centimeter of it.

From the free world would come a cake vendor, and with the cakes he also brought the sweetness of gambling. Two of us would pay him ten groszy, five groszy each, then he would rattle his coins in the pocket of his dirty apron, take out a handful, and say, "Odd or even." The boy who guessed correctly got the cake and ate it on the spot. I wasn't allowed to eat them; my father said I could get food poisoning. I didn't disobey him, although somehow all my classmates remained in perfect health.

For several meters along the wall of the building ran a concrete rainspout from the hill, and we wore out our shoes climbing up and sliding down it endlessly, that is, until the bell for class. We also loosened all the iron rails in the stone posts, and we tore (I almost said "gnawed") the bark off the trees around the playing field. In other words, we were a kind of collective Abbot Faria from a Dumas novel. If you could somehow concentrate the energy of all the schoolchildren in the world, you could definitely turn the earth upside down and dry up all the seas. But first you would have to make that absolutely forbidden.

I have sketched something like outlines here for essays entitled "The Gymnasium as Subculture" and "The Gymnasium as Elemental Force." But we were also a society, governing ourselves with a legal system, a democratically elected chieftain, a treasury and treasurer, which I was for a time, sergeants at arms in the classrooms, and a hierarchy that included two special positions: the mama's boy and the class jester. The mama's boy was determined by class verdict, unofficial but without appeal. The ideal candidate was fat and clumsy, someone you could mistreat a little—not with any cruelty but simply to remind him what he was. If he accepted his role, he could lead a perfectly reasonable existence. As a rule a class had only one mama's boy, as if having more than one would reflect unfavorably on the group itself. In our class, for many years this position was filled by two, but the exception proved the rule, because they were twins, the F. brothers, forming one person, as it were, in two bodies: one mama's boy, except doubled. Our verdict led to a curious fraternal rivalry, setting one against the other. More than once, after long whispering in the corner, they would come to blows, but as mama's boys, of course, swinging wildly, pulling hair, and blubbering. When the twins were ill, the position fell *per procura* to fat Z. He was incredibly touchy, had perfect cheeks for pinching, and, being both fat and standoffish, was a natural for squashing. Squashing involved two athletes, who would sit on the bench on either side of the unsuspecting victim—you couldn't squash without a bench—and at a given signal they would plant their feet and grip the desk and press the poor soul between them until his ribs made sounds and his eyeballs popped. But the mama's boy was not persecuted too insistently—that was considered poor taste.

Looking more closely at this school society, one may notice a certain anxiety among some students, who know instinctively that they are candidates for the position of mama's boy and will surely be pushed into it if it becomes vacant. These are the ones who persecute the most, as if to separate themselves with punches and insults from what they dread to be. Meanwhile worthy representatives of the class take no interest in its pariahs.

You became a mama's boy by decree and consensus, but you became a class jester by native ability and the ambition to be one. A class jester could amuse the class with a single word at the right moment, knew how to coin a phrase, but most of all knew how to be stupid when called on by the teacher. A difficult position, for it demanded balance between the class and the enemy camp. You couldn't be the jester of both, either. To keep an acrobatic act like that going was no simple art.

In our class Miecio P. was jester for a while, a boy of heavy humor and a heavier hand. Questioned, he played the idiot in such a way as to make the questioner look like an idiot. He was merciless particularly to the young women who assisted the teachers and sometimes conducted classes themselves. Miecio was vulgar, and I didn't like him. He sat on the last bench and often pretended to be hard of hearing, so the questions would have to be repeated, and

he lied in a special way, giving detailed but completely absurd explanations for not having done his homework, while
staring at the teacher with unabashed sincerity. The more
obvious the lie, the more detailed the account. He evoked
laughter, but any laughter at him personally was cut short
by a pointed nod at the gang he belonged to. These were
repeat offenders and athletic types the pedagogues had
given up on. Miecio was their spokesman, even their intellectual, but not their leader, because they didn't appre-
ciate humor and kept their distance, like visitors from a
world outside the gymnasium. To them we were kids. One
of them, for example, W., would let this one or that try to
strangle him, hands around his throat, and resist with nothing but the boardlike tightening of his neck muscles.

While we in the middle grades began to take an interest
in sexual matters, outdoing one another in verbal pornog-
raphy and scatology, the eloquence of which attempted to
substitute for experience, this gang did not join in such
discussions. Sex for them was an everyday thing, routine,
practically a profession. With despair we shouted the most
dreadful obscenities, feeling the ground of desired mascu-
linity slipping out from under our feet.

Curiously, I remember their hands and book bags better
than their faces. The hands were the hands of grown
men—heavy and still, with yellow nicotine stains, protrud-
ing veins, scars, but not scars from some penknife in a
game; their scars had nothing to do with games. The book
bags were leather worn to a muddy black, torn, without
handles, the sides half fallen in, because they didn't hold
much besides lunch, and you could see that for years they
had been put to the roughest service—used as goals in

truant soccer games, as pillows in the Kaiserwald, even as missiles. Such a veteran book bag deserves to be placed in the museum alongside the old school bench.

There were many classmates I was on good terms with, but I had no real friends to whom I could confide my private thoughts. I liked Jozek F., who started getting a mustache I think as early as the first year of the new gymnasium. He was an excellent mathematician—killed by the Germans. I was also impressed by Zygmunt E., called Puncia. Oddly, I remember him not at a desk or in a classroom but on the playing field. A son of poor parents, he worked his way through the gymnasium by tutoring. Tuition was expensive—110 zlotys a semester, the equivalent of a suit or five pairs of shoes—and scholarships were hard to come by. I remember Puncia—a dramatic, heroic moment— making a penalty kick before the opposing goal. He placed the ball eleven paces from the goal, while the goalie, crouched and staring, nervously licked his lips. Then Puncia retreated and stood in silent, almost mournful thought, his eyes narrowed, as if struggling with his opponent, and his body tensed slightly. He began moving toward the ball, running slowly at first, waddling like a duck because his legs were a little crooked, and he also moved them in a special way to keep the goalie from guessing which leg he would kick with. We all knew which leg—it was always the left—yet surprisingly this game of pretended uncertainty always worked. In the last few meters he gathered speed, until his legs were a blur; then came the dull thud of the kick, and the ball went right into the corner of the goal. In the uproar of our triumph Puncia would turn slowly and smile. It was the same smile he showed in the classroom, polite, sweet, mild, and completely uninterested.

For many years I had two neighbors in class. One was Julek C., the son of a policeman, a sturdy kid with blond hair, a snub nose, and a tentative expression in his eyes. He and I carried out an important transaction which took a long time to finalize. He gave me his single-shot 6mm pistol in exchange for my fake Browning 9mm, with which I was bored. Of course I wanted to try out the gun right away; every minute was precious. So the moment I was home, I loaded it with a "ball." It was hard to fit the thing into the chamber, but I managed. I opened the window in the room by the kitchen, aimed at the bathroom door at the end of the hall, and fired. The bang was unexpectedly loud; I would even say horrendous. Before I could go and see what had happened to the bullet, my mother came running in and, after her, my father, from his office, in his white lab coat, the mirror on his forehead. My still-smoking gun was immediately confiscated, and it ended up in a double-locked drawer as a highly dangerous object. Much later, I examined it and realized that I had been lucky, because the firing chamber was of thin metal and part of it had been expanded by the hot gases. Fortunately the flexible copper held and it didn't all go into my eyes. I looked for the bullet a long time, in vain; the bore apparently had not been rifled. So Julek got the better of the bargain after all. It may have been a family thing with him, but we talked a lot about guns. He was even in a hunt once, for wild boar, and was wounded in the thigh when a hunter aimed at a boar he thought he saw in the bushes. Julek wore a bandage for a long time, which was a great distinction. But that happened later, at the lyceum. By then Julek D. also had a gun, a magnificent Flower repeating rifle, whereas I never went beyond my air pistol. This stung deeply. Had it been up to me, I would have gone to school with revolvers hung all over myself. At best I could make certificates of hunting prowess for myself, but I did this halfheartedly, feeling that in that particular area fiction could not compete at all with reality.

Even earlier, my desk neighbor was Jurek G., handsome and amorous. He was always romantically involved with girls, and in addition—supposedly—was having an actual affair with a grown woman, a widow. He met her in Stryjski Park, they said, and one of my classmates reportedly observed him there in the throes of passion, but there was no way I could observe, too, because I was carefully watched. In the afternoon I was not allowed to leave the house; I was given a guardian angel, my tutor Mr. Wilk, a student and then a graduate student in law. He made sure I did my homework. Therefore the classical excuse, "I'm going to a friend's to study," was ruled out for me: I really did have to study. Also I was learning French at home, from a certain Mademoiselle, an ugly person with an enormous red nose that was pitted, as if under a magnifying glass. But I was able to tame her, working out a whole system of stratagems to deliver me from the mysteries of that horrible grammar. Mademoiselle was very inquisitive and would ask me about my family, ask if someone was getting married or not getting married; knowing next to nothing about such matters, I lied, saying whatever entered my head—and so managed to *parler* a little after all, but the secrets of tenses, *temps défini, indéfini,* and all those awful *subjonctifs* remained hidden from me forever.

At that time I was making my own alcoholic beverages —in case male guests dropped in unexpectedly, though they never did. Behind the volumes of the Brockhaus and Meyer encyclopedia in the dirty white cabinet, I hid tiny bottles filled with leftover drinks mixed according to my own recipe. I used ingredients from my mother's cupboard, adding them to the kümmel my father sometimes had with lunch. When I ran out of family gossip, I would treat my French teacher to one of these cocktails, and she was not above accepting a little glass or two. On tiny porcelain saucers from my chemical experiments I also mixed perfumes taken from my mother's dresser. And I would anoint Mademoiselle with these. It is amazing that after all this I can read a book in the language of Molière.

Between school, Mr. Wilk, and the French teacher, I didn't have much time to myself, and my life would have been dreary indeed if I hadn't enriched it in hidden ways, but more of that later.

There was some diversion in the school plays, though many, like Wyspianski's *Liberation*, were awful bores (I am speaking not of Wyspianski himself but only of his reception among fourteen-year-olds at the time). The tickets, numbered, were distributed in class, and immediately there would be a lively discussion about where the girls' gymnasium would sit. Through secret channels came valuable information, and bargaining and trading ensued, since practically everyone wanted to sit where you could count on a voluptuous neighbor. This didn't concern me; I was still infantile and green and could do no more than listen with an open mouth as Jurek G. spoke of his rendezvous and all that transpired during them. Anyway, at the school plays no real advantage derived from female proximity, because strategically placed teachers made sure that not even the slightest contact took place.

From time to time there were dances arranged by the parents' committee, but I still didn't know how to dance and could only stand by a wall, that is, by the risers, since the dancing was in the gym. Some of the younger teachers, too, danced with our guests of the fair sex—which to me seemed against nature. As if Attila were to take up ballet.

To describe my position in the class, I must compare it to others. Although clumsy and quite pudgy, I somehow didn't become a mama's boy. Perhaps because I kept my distance, was a good student, and had a lot of things on my mind. I believe it was at the end of gymnasium or the beginning of lyceum that I encountered Proust, learning of his existence from Jeremi R. and Janek C. Jeremi was studying English, carried dictionaries with him, and in general was extraordinarily intelligent. Because I read absolutely everything that fell into my hands, and saw that Janek and Jeremi had books with intriguing titles, such as *Within a Budding Grove*, I borrowed the first volume—and got stuck in the first few pages. Surprised, I stepped back like a hurdler to gather momentum and charged the obstacle a few times, but each time I fell back as if I had hit a wall. Maybe it was this that planted the seeds of my inferiority complex. I tried reading Proust but couldn't—but I couldn't even try going out with girls. I had to pretend this was by choice, pretend even before my friends, including Janek C. How I envied him! He was the son of a well-

known Lvov lawyer and lived not far from us, off Mickiewicz Avenue, near Smolka Square, in a large apartment.
Entering, the visitor would be greeted by a Roman bust of
Janek's father, a powerful head on a massive neck, a craggy
face, wide nostrils. Janek's mother had mental problems.
He never spoke of her. She stayed in the apartment in a
separate room, the door almost always closed. The few
times I saw her there, for a moment, the air was blue with
smoke and she held a cigarette. Janek did not have a tutor.
In general, his father treated him like an adult; Janek didn't
have to say where he was going or what he wanted to do
or if he had finished his homework. He would read Proust,
wearing his wire-rimmed glasses. When I came, he closed
the book and took off the glasses, along with a piece of
paper kept under the frame so the wire wouldn't leave a
mark. He was an excellent swimmer, could do one hundred
meters freestyle in a minute and sixteen seconds (whereas
I, in the water, splashed and went nowhere); he played ten-
nis, basketball, and in lyceum dated the beautiful Wanda
P., which he never discussed. He never boasted of his su-
periorities. But what impressed me most about him was
that, an average student, he did not take school too seriously, did not fear bad grades, as if he could see farther, as
if he had his own system of values and was practicing it
quietly. We walked each other home, between Brajerska
and Mickiewicz. Janek was a good, obliging person with a
somewhat lethargic manner and a great sense of humor. I
believe that he, too, was killed by the Germans.

In gymnasium I did many things not because I liked doing them but because they were what my peers did (in this,
following the adults, although I didn't know that). Even

before lyceum, my more sophisticated classmates began to play bridge, which to me seemed worse than irregular Latin verbs. I could never remember what cards had been played, what was in my hand, what to bid, and how to open. Considered retarded by my partners, I gave up bridge once and for all. As for chess, I actually did win once against a boy my age who was an outstanding player—and won in a way that stunned him. A feat I was never able to repeat. I think this was a situation such as Napoleon spoke about—to the effect that on the field of battle the most dangerous opponent is either a strategic genius or a complete cretin, and that sometimes the cretin has the advantage, since his moves cannot be foreseen.

For a while I played buttons, swiping some valuable specimens from my mother's dresser, and in class I threw spit-soaked cigarette butts at the ceiling—everyone did that. When the spit dried, the butts began to fall in a mysterious rain during the lecture, which infuriated the teacher. I studied jujitsu with Janek C., usually in the third-floor lavatory vestibule, and hurled special darts at the blackboard—made of cork with a needle in front and feathers and a microscopic weight in back. I learned how to spit five, even six meters, but not how to whistle with fingers, which was one of my great aggravations. If I failed at things in this education, if things were beyond my grasp, it was not for lack of trying. I strove to conform—for example, pretending to collect stamps, which didn't interest me in the least, and with my friends who did visit I played soldiers and war, not looking at my notebooks until I was alone.

But going to the Eastern Fair, for that I didn't have to force myself. We went in a group, and collected the free-coupon flyers and drank the free Maggi soup until the managers of the stands lost all patience and drove us away.

My obesity proved to be an advantage in certain situations, such as when I played defense in soccer and it was difficult to push me aside in the scrimmage because I had a lot of mass. And on rare occasions there were car races in Lvov, which we loved with a passion. They made a loop using Stryjska, Cadet, and Pelczynska streets; they even poured plaster over the tram tracks and put sandbags at the sidewalk corners. We felt then that Lvov was an exceptionally European city, and the proof was those enormous racing machines and the hellish roar they made.

I confess with some embarrassment that I never played hooky, but sometimes a class was canceled and we went to Highcastle, Kortumowa Mountain, or the Kaiserwald. I got to know that area better in the winter, on skis, and also as a member of the Cadet Corps—the fallen trees, ravines, hills. But the best view was from the Memorial Mound of the Lublin Union.

CHAPTER

5

THE DIRECTOR OF our school was Stanislaw Bu-
zath, a small man with a big, commanding voice, but
he was also a good historian and a decent person. Geography was taught by Professor Nawrocki, called the Conductor because he silenced us with a special bell, pushing
a button in his office. Lewicki and Bleiberg took turns
teaching physics. I was once given a good smack by the
former while he was lecturing on the properties of mercury,
because I sat in the first row and in my eagerness to impress
him with my knowledge completed all his sentences for

him. He hit me so hard that I saw stars. A terrible disappointment: I had hoped to be singled out in another way. Miss Maria Lewicka, his namesake but no relative, taught Polish. I was always first in that class, and wrote long compositions, hardly ever able to finish them in the allotted forty-five minutes. She wrote many wonderful comments in red ink in my notebook—especially when the topic was open. That was my favorite kind of composition. Alas, I abused my special position by rarely studying or preparing for class. From the required reading list I chose only what I liked, and the Szymonowiczes and Kasprowiczes were ignored. Hence my gaps in Polish literature, which were not always filled later. I took advantage of the fact that Lewicka never called on me, and now present the sad case of a man who has been graduated from college but does not know the first thing about grammar, for in that subject I was negligent, spoiled by the confidence placed in me. Once, writing a homework assignment, I did a shameful thing. On my voyage to the planet Venus—that was the theme, which combined the requirements of composition with my own interests—I lifted a large chunk of text from a book by Professor Wyrobek on the wonders of nature: in striking prose, a description of Venus with its primal jungles and thick clouds. So my literary career began, in gymnasium, with a simple act of plagiarism. I think I did try to add something of my own, some nonsense about the Venusians (the errors of youth, how they take their revenge in later years!), but saw it was inferior to the expressiveness and vividness of Professor Wyrobek's vision. Our Polish teacher conducted her classes in the modern way, encouraging free discussion. Having owned up to some sins, I wish to balance the picture a little by adding here that I was not indifferent to everything in Polish class, that it was not just on "Venusian" topics that I had things to say. Lewicka's method encouraged independent thinking. On the other hand, it required a little cooperation and industry from the student, and not every student was up to that.

Mathematics was taught by Professor Zarycki, one of the more unusual members of the faculty, a Ukrainian whose daughter was involved in the assassination attempt on Minister Pieracki. Zarycki was probably in his fifties, handsome, with a furrowed, swarthy face, even swarthier eyelids, a sharp nose, deep eyes, and he was bald as a billiard ball, because he carefully shaved his skull. The class was terribly afraid of him, and I was as well, because mathematics was my nemesis. Our mathematician treated us strangely—he had an imagination. He might reward a correct answer by telling the student to leave the classroom and go for a walk around the city. Or he might begin the lesson by sending some students to different places, on various personal errands. Which was a great favor—an unusually safe way to exclude oneself from the dangers that lay in wait on the chalk-scribbled blackboard. Zarycki resembled the film actor Boris Karloff in that he never smiled and no emotion showed on his masklike face. Sometimes he would give a particularly hard question to the whole class and offer a cigarette to the one who answered correctly. Once, thanks to an unexpected inspiration, I received such a trophy and carried it triumphantly home. I didn't smoke this cigarette, of course; I kept it until the tobacco started to crumble. Zarycki was frightening because he was enigmatic—nobody could tell when he was joking and when he was in earnest. When a new student, answering well and hearing that he could go for a walk in the town, returned instead to his seat, Zarycki let out such a bellow that the boy fled as fast as he could. What kind of man was this really? I have no idea. What did we know about any of our teachers? We were taught by Professor Ingarden, also mathematics; even then he was a philosopher of European renown, but in our school nobody knew that. Ingarden didn't stay long or devote much effort to us, and no wonder, since our collective resistance to mathematics was more than a match for the greatest pedagogical talent.

The great, eccentric teacher is dying out as a species, it seems, because conditions have become unfavorable for him. Nawrocki the Conductor was replaced temporarily by a newcomer from another gymnasium, Babyn, who within a single hour destroyed the entire class, this with one trick question: "How many continents are there?" If you answered "Five," you got an F. F followed F followed F. Finally he explained that there were five continents on Earth, yes, but many more in the whole universe. There was of course no arguing with that, so on my report card I received an unsatisfactory in geography, though with plenty of company. Babyn was a terror; everyone feared him, because those who studied found themselves in the same boat as those who never touched a book. I know nothing about him; he appeared like a comet of devastation and not long after, a few months, passed from our small horizon, having turned hours of geography into sessions of horror. I suspect that he was not quite right in the head, because the victories he won against us were such cheap ones.

The lower grades of Latin were taught by Professor Rappaport—old, ailing, a yellow face, a gruff but gentle disposition. He hardly ever left the lectern, so during his reign the illegal transmission of correct answers flowered greatly. But even then we were beginning to hear disturbing stories about another Latin teacher, Auerbach, and the time came, in one of the higher grades, when he manifested himself in the flesh.

Short of stature and comical in appearance, Auerbach would come to school in enormous galoshes, which he removed from his feet with ferocious kicks at the entrance to the classroom. Then, to have better command of the room, he would hop up on the podium table, let his legs dangle, and in the dead silence look at us carefully through his thick glasses. After a few minutes of this hypnotic watching, he would find the student least prepared for danger, and if the victim made even the feeblest gesture of soliciting the help of his neighbors, Auerbach would spring tigerlike and appear suddenly beside the prey, examining his desk, book, hands. The man was a true detective in spotting sinners. During quizzes he did not take refuge in the fortress of his desk but moved silently about the room. His bloodcurdling battle cry, "A-hee!," which was a little nasal, and all the special intonations and expressions he used to skewer a culprit were imitated by us endlessly and mocked; but that didn't break the terrible spell cast by our little Latin teacher. My guess is that at the very beginning of his teaching career he realized that he would have to compensate in some very definite, dramatic way for the physical inadequacies of his person—his extreme nearsightedness, his dwarfism making him laughable, vulnerable. So he worked out a whole system of ambushes, sorties, leaps, and thundering, and that was his shield. Basically he was an intelligent, peaceable man. I remember how upset he became when, at the fourth-year graduation, one of our classmates, U., who had grown too big for his uniform, saw all the Fs on the certificate handed him by the gymnasium authorities, pulled a flask from his pocket, threw his head back, and drank the contents in two gulps, the smell of iodine spreading all around. . . . Everyone stood rooted in horror, Auerbach probably most of all, his F being the final nail in U.'s coffin. After a few minutes of confusion it turned out that the liquid was not lethal—just water with a few drops of tincture of iodine in it. U., who didn't care anymore, had chosen this colorful way to conclude his stay at our school.

In the language of the ancient Romans I was not particularly adept, but I had a sense of rhythm and could read an unfamiliar text in hexameter without understanding— nota bene—any of it. Perhaps the fluency of my speech and correctness of my accents softened somewhat the injury done to the Latin teachers' ears by my less eloquent fellow students. The teachers liked me. In addition, I never dared use a crib. Many of my classmates did, of course, in the conviction that homework was not their first duty. Thus they added to that great storehouse of subterfuges used for centuries by students in the war against education. The smuggling of information—the essential purpose of all such activity—called for the creation of many industries. First, the handicrafts, painstaking artisan work. I have in mind the insertion of a translation, say, between the lines of Latin text, and marking the caesuras, the long and short syllables, the dactyls, trochees, this done by placing a piece of paper over the page and writing the letters and words in pencil, bearing down so that the crib would be in the form only of colorless indentations. Holding the book at the exact angle to the light, you could read—particularly with young eyes—the lifesaving information. If you didn't want to go to so much trouble, you could make use of the products of an unscrupulous publisher, I think it was Zuckerkandel, who printed small yellow ponies that were available in all the gymnasiums of Lvov and no doubt throughout Poland. These were translations as well as parsings of the required Latin texts, poems, and plays, printed on cheap paper and in tiny type. Possession of a pony was a heinous crime; therefore the more cautious of us copied onto small strips of paper the parts of the Latin translation needed, and hid them in pockets and up sleeves. But there were plenty who were too lazy and simply tore the appropriate page from the Zuckerkandel and put it in the textbook. Others counted on their height, towering over Auerbach and holding the textbook high so he could not see it. Fools. Our incredible sleuth could tell from the eye movements that skulduggery was afoot, and the consequence was a sudden paralyzing cry of "A-hee!" and a leap from the podium, and the dry teacher's hand seizing the book, and the secret sin revealed to the class, the page of the pony, which Auerbach would wave in all directions like a cloth dipped in poison, wave it with disgust and bitter triumph. And if the page was hidden in time, passed to a colleague, the little teacher would quickly order the whole row emptied, and one by one pull from the desks all that they held. Such searches usually ended sadly.

Of course, various countermeasures were attempted, new methods used. You could read from a crib held at a certain angle by a student sitting in the row in front of you, he hiding it from Auerbach with an open book. But our indefatigable master of detection easily scotched such trickery. There was visionary talk of using a mirror to throw messages on a wall, as a film projector did, in a corner behind the teacher's back, in Morse code. Nothing came of that, because in the end it was easier to learn a translation by ordinary means than to master the art of a telegraphic alphabet.

Writing about my teachers, I feel with growing dissatisfaction that I have fallen into one of the many ruts made by generations of professional memoirists, where one speaks of the gymnasium as a dollhouse—from above, at a distance, with a sad smile, the pedagogues presented in gentle, forgiving caricature. The tired tricks of a balding writer! Tricks all the more insidious in that they are unconscious, turning prose into a sweet pabulum, a candied mud that gums and paralyzes the mind. To write about the gymnasium from above is worse than a crime—it's a mistake. One should treat it as one treats the Absolute.

Fortified by walls and chalk, the gymnasium existed basically in the faculty body—this would be the first approximation. I am quite serious. Teachers from other schools —one met them in the theater, for example—to us they were as heretics are to the orthodox, they and their altars and practices. We felt embarrassment, surprise: there was absolutely nothing to them; how could they be so blind? At a glance I could reduce any foreign schoolmaster to his elements, from galoshes to official abstractedness to pince-nez. He was the tedious sum of his parts, nothing more. But the fact that our Conductor had a big belly never entered my head—because he was an Absolute, he and his notebook and little pencil of power and the way his fingers slowly turned those always mysterious pages, pages that one minute were as empty as the world before creation and the next full of silent thunder. Prophets in the front row would try to read our implacable fate in the microscopic movements of that pencil. More than once I carried the test books to the conference room. There must have been a table there, chairs, but I have no memory of them. As for the director's office, I couldn't begin to describe it, and that is not solely because of the circumstances that brought me there (for example, the time L. and I broke the lavatory sink). It was not fear that blinded me, but the Absolute. The Absolute was there; I could feel it. Years later, I even looked for it when, as a man of letters, I was to meet students in the first and second gymnasiums and waited, with coffee, in the director's office. I found nothing; it had evaporated like camphor, leaving the desks cold, the chairs and coat of arms and portraits on the wall—it was gone, but gone only for me. Its presence I immediately saw reflected in the faces of the students when they crossed the threshold. Immediately they fell into that trance so familiar to me. I recognized the slight numbing, stiffening, trembling, the dark exultation in the eyes, the failing of all the senses—they did not speak to the point and shuffled their feet. As I once did. Out of fear? Their fear, and mine, at twelve? Too simple! When the Germans were shelling Lvov in September, I ran through Jesuit Garden looking for still-hot shrapnel timers—in terrible fear, because the bombardment continued—and the point is not that I was stupid but that the danger was trivially definite: a shell could kill. The director, on the other hand, not only didn't kill but often didn't even raise his voice.

I know that describing some things is like trying to square the circle; that the believer, while faith lasts, neither wishes nor is able to speak of his faith, for its state, like the possession of ears or legs, is not communicable. The atheist debunks the mysticism of his old memories by faultfinding analysis or the tolerant superiority of one awakened from a dream. Go ahead, gentlemen, analyze, smile your sad smiles, weave your comfortable tale of the past. I cannot join you. Mysticism? Yes, but of a special kind, an Absolute that is omnipresent yet at the same time wholly material. The tribes of the gymnasium do not hold with superstition, do not believe in telepathy or mind over matter. They would master both if the world allowed it. No spiritualist is more attuned to the minds of others or whispers from the beyond than we were to a drop of knowledge, eye to eye at the blackboard with the Absolute, the burning Sahara of ignorance in our heads. As for psychokinesis, we were forty joined in spirit, and quicker than it takes to read this sentence, the teacher, the lectern, and his notes would have plunged through all the floors below if thought strained to the utmost could indeed move matter.

My style waxes biblical, but perhaps one can speak of such things only thus. Or should I instead become Homeric? The Ancient Greeks made fun of their gods, knowing their weaknesses and foibles. Even the Jews of the Old Testament, when God turned His head, started whispering in the corners, playing hooky with golden calves, losing faith in their teacher's podium, the Ark of the Covenant. An Ezekiel could deliver an algebra lesson in numbered verse, each line containing a soul-shaking bolt; I won't attempt that. Whatever I do, it will verge on a joke, a parody, and yet the *spiritus* that *flat ubi vult* filled with high-voltage transcendence the piece of chalk held in stiff fingers that awaited the Word. Have I exaggerated? No, I did not consider our math teacher a god, nor the director a Zeus. Nevertheless, after all these years and wars, many of my old classmates still dream of final exams every bit as terrible as the Last Judgment, though no Goya has painted their eschatology. Are we to dismiss the evidence of our senses and stubborn dreams with such words as "awe of authority"? I know only this: We were forced to learn and fought it like the plague, but at the same time we were initiated into ultimate experience, and from minds tuned in unison the highest and lowest human notes were produced. Yes, there was Old Testament quaking before the burning bush, and terror before the fire and brimstone of Fs, and with more than one teacher we argued like Moses on Sinai when he was called on unexpectedly by Jehovah. Those feelings took us past all we knew and placed us painfully face to face with the Unknowable, that divine element, that hideous ecstasy, which I, free of it for so many years, now try to invoke with the name of the Absolute.

Each of us in the course of a lifetime grows out of a series of faiths, abandoning their temples, but the things toppled from the pedestals of yesterday's cult deserve neither our contempt nor our affection. I will say more: I didn't know this then, but our teachers would have been nothing without us, in the frame of erasers and black roll books and carved desks; it was from the interaction between us and them that there gradually emerged something that sanctified and gave power to their spectacles, galoshes, watch chains, and little pencils. When the bubble burst and everything vanished behind the walls of the gymnasium like a magic circle when it is crossed, what remained was a vague impression, a thing impossible to verbalize and which memories attempt to show in vain, for besides the hours of instruction and the pandemonium of recesses I knew a certain condition born of relationships only half visible, a condition that may have dwindled to insignificance in the perspective of time and also may have been a little grotesque—open to laughter when the sleeper woke—but it was my first initiation into the tragicomedy of existence. There were other initiations, because later, too, I experienced the rise, flowering, and fall of mighty principles that eventually turned out to be—as in all histories, large and small—ordinary people. The thunderbolt held by Zeus in the textbook of ancient history always reminded me of a twist of Carpathian goat cheese. I beheld it without illusion—as today I behold the precisely sharpened little pencil of the Conductor. Olympus, for the one who has awakened, is only a mountain and requires hiking boots, not sacrificial animals. In gymnasium directors' offices there is nothing for me now but desks and chairs; I say this without sorrow but also without a smile, for that is the way of things.

After which harangue I return to Lvov of the thirties, to its shady walkways and hilly streets, the green, almost sylvan Academic Street, Legions Street bracketed by the Grand Theater and with Mariacki Square in the middle, gorgeous at night with the rooftop lights—the stag of

Schicht's soap, the Suchard chocolates hopping on their neon ladder. Around 1935, a talking film came, Al Jolson and his title song "Sonny Boy," which the street singers immediately took up. The streets and courtyards then were filled with jugglers, fire-eaters, acrobats, singers and musicians, and the most authentic organ grinders in the world, some even with parrots that could tell the future by picking cards with their beaks. I don't know whether it is from a guilty conscience because of my murdered music box, but the hobbling, twanging, awkward, always slightly off-key music of all organ grinders and other anachronistic mechanisms is something I hold in great respect. There is in it a sweet, naive solemnity, a nineteenth-century trust in the perfection of wheels and toothed cylinders, and an honesty of mechanical matter speaking in its own voice instead of imitating the human. But the Heraclitean river has claimed all those hand-cranked clunkers and clangers.

I also loved to watch circus performers from the kitchen steps. Sometimes whole families put on a show; they traveled with frayed canvas suitcases that contained torches, weights, a sword for swallowing, a rolled carpet to do acrobatic tricks on, and other curiosities. While the paterfamilias ate fire or a sword, the mother played the accordion, and the children made human pyramids and ran about the courtyard picking up the coins wrapped in paper, thrown from the windows. Those were hard times, and poverty put into the street not only the circus but also trade and manufacturing. There was a multitude of peddlers selling combs and mirrors, and one often heard the bells of the knife grinders and their cry, "Pots soldered!" And there were Gypsy women who told fortunes, and out-and-out beggars who had nothing to sell, only their misery. All these figures were to me a natural part of the city—as if it could not be otherwise.

Of the talking films I really remember only the ones with monsters: King Kong, the four-story ape who fell in love with a lady, climbed a skyscraper, grabbed her through a window, removed her clothes, then held her in his hand like a banana. And the Mummy, the Black Room, the Werewolf. In *The Mummy*, Boris Karloff, playing the mummy, put his hand on the arm of the young Egyptologist; that five-fingered ruin straight from the grave was terrible, a masterpiece of makeup. Karloff was incomparable in the role of spastic corpses (*Frankenstein* and *Son of Frankenstein*). The films somehow went in families, because right after that I saw *Son of King Kong*. A noble ape, friendly toward humans on a volcanic island, when the ocean swallows the island, holds the heroes above water in his hand until a ship comes, but the ape himself, after his good deed, sinks with bubbles to the bottom.

In the theater I had the unpleasant habit of jabbing my father with an elbow during the more gripping scenes, and in certain films I would hit him nonstop. Reprimands didn't help; this was stronger than I was. The more afraid I got, the more I liked it; the less afraid, the less I liked it. Why we enjoy being frightened (within reason) is a mystery, and I have no explanation for it.

Like every Lvov child, I visited the Raclawicka Panorama, a great attraction. The entrance itself put you in an elevated mood, because you walked through a dim place and after a flight of stairs came out on a bridge that was exactly like being suspended in the gondola of a giant motionless balloon. From this bridge you saw the panorama of a battle as real as life, and there was a lot of argument about where the authentic fence (with jugs set on poles) ended and the painting of the fence began. At that time I had no problem with the naturalistic school of art. I liked going to the theater early, before the enormous metal curtain painted by Siemiradzki went up, there were so many entertaining things depicted on it. Our Grand Theater seemed to me an incredibly luxurious place, *comme il faut*, in the best taste, with its red velvet upholstery, the many floors, the candelabras, the smoking room, and—last but not least—the buffet, where my father would buy my mother and me pieces of thinly sliced ham. I don't recall what outstanding dramatic works I saw there but remember perfectly that a piece of ham cost fifty groszy.

I was growing civilized, to the best of my ability, yet deep within I was on the side of all those forces against which civilization struggles. Proof of this: my reaction to severe winters and other, more temporary, disasters. Lvov weather was mild; a winter storm there was virtually unknown. But in 1930, I believe, with the sky as clear as a blue iceberg, the temperature fell to twenty-six below; the price of fuel soared; huddled children ran after every coal wagon, waiting for a piece to drop off. When my father and I went for a walk—I wrapped to a ridiculous degree in thick felts and earmuffs—we would pass several large iron baskets in which was burning coal provided by the city, and around each basket some of the frozen warmed themselves a little. This all seemed wonderful to me, and I hoped even more for catastrophic changes when the snowstorm came. I hoped that the snow would bury our house, that all the trams and automobiles would stop, that I would be able to step from our third-floor balcony right into a street that was a canyon of ice. Similarly, when there was a rare electrical outage, I would help search for candles with reverence, would carry their tentative, unsteady light through the house, which had become suddenly blind and mysteriously spacious. And how sad I was when the vulgar light bulbs came on again, ending the sweet magic of that medieval dark!

AS MUCH AS I have spoken about the events that filled my childhood, I still feel I have not discharged the debt I owe them. The "laying of the psyche's foundation" is how I would name that first gathering of experience from commerce with the world, and in time it is revealed to be unexchangeable with any other. Because of this "foundation" you can be a materialist and atheist twenty times over and still feel a stirring in your gut when you hear organ music or the ringing of bells—while the voice of the muezzin calling the faithful to prayer may be attractive and exotic but remains foreign to you. Indeed, this is the initiation into the concrete shape of your culture, which is more enduring than any system of faith, because you can know perfectly well that there are different kinds of cemeteries in the world, but the "real" cemetery will always be the one with tombstones hidden in wild thyme and crosses of stone and birch tilted at angles as if pushed by the wind. But the laying of the psyche's foundation is also the establishing of the most tender ties, because they are the first, with the prosaic products of civilization. For what poetry, really, inhered in the long Haberbusch beer wagons, their kegs secured by hooks, their heavy draft horses glossy from oats? Or in the old automobiles that, climbing Cadet or Stryjska Street, groaned and shuddered so, you not only felt their desperate effort but had to assist them by exerting all your will? Those wrecks demanded your constant attention, sympathy, I would even say acts of charity, which today's cars, designed to conceal proudly from their drivers the extent of their effort, neither ask of us nor require. Those old vehicles, now antiques, were by their very undependability true individuals.

I remember my introduction to the automotive art. A year before I graduated, I was given an instructor of few words who looked as if he subsisted entirely on black oil. The first lesson was how to crank the motor, and, since motors kicked like restive horses, he began by showing me how to hold the handle so a sudden kick wouldn't break my wrist. And when I finally sat on the leather seat, which stank of gasoline, the man told me—and in that moment he resembled Captain Nemo when he commanded the *Nautilus* through the terrifying Arabian Tunnel—to put the car in first and drive full speed toward the brick wall of the courtyard. Deliciously faint with fear, I obeyed, and with the mad rush of a charging soldier we made for the red wall. A meter from it, my preceptor used his own separate brake. In those days the synchronization of gears was considered an unhealthy debauchery thought up by foreign fops; the ignition was done by hand, the horn was a rubber bulb like an enema syringe, and to change a tire you needed the strength of Hercules.

But the domestic area of life, too, not yet touched by

the bacillus of indolent automation, presented itself to me in the full wealth of its liturgical schedule. I have already mentioned the cataclysm of Laundry Day, which was divided into the soapsuds-and-steam phase, the backbreaking scrubbing-in-tubs phase, and finally the wringing phase, which shook the whole house with wooden clatter. And the marathons run in place, on brushes, to turn the floor into a mirror. And the ironing in a cloud of fumes, when the ironing woman would keep running to the porch and waving the iron to make the coals burn, and sparks would fly from the half-moon slits in the sides as if from the belly of a locomotive. And the periodic visits of the seamstress, who rattled on the machine from morning till night, while I made off with scraps of cloth because I wasn't supposed to. And the cooking of the jam and my persistent request to be promoted to collect—with a large wooden spoon—the froth from the volcanic pool of raspberry. The froth belonged on a plate, according to my mother, but my clever design was for it to end up instead in my salivating mouth. The rational purpose of all this hard labor was unimportant. Its primitive nature indeed consumed an enormous amount of time and strength—but because of that primitive nature my childhood was given an apprenticeship in forces fundamentally disobedient. When sparks burned black holes in clothing or the jam in the cupboard turned to sugar or went moldy, I learned about the stubbornness of an only half-tamed Nature, which bubbled on the stove and blazed in the oven. And even if nothing catastrophic happened, the house was changed, and I lived now in proximity to doom, seeing how careful one had to be with the harnessing of processes trapped in pots and tubs, unpredictable processes, like sailing on an unknown sea. The power that lay in yellowing grandmother-recipes was summoned so that the laundry could be a pretty bluish white, and so that the fruit could keep its shape while the syrup it swam in took on the color of old wine. But sometimes experience was not enough. Nothing was sure or automatic; it was always married to risk. The roses were kept in baskets, and the whitish tip of each petal was removed with small scissors, and then there was more pre-jam activity, the Danaidean froth and the magic-more-than-chemistry of sterilizing the glass, until finally this mountain of labor produced a row of labeled jars that turned the cupboard into a glorious museum. So I understand perfectly the mixture of contempt and fear in the breast of those housekeepers of yore (where are they today?) when they learned that industry could equal them in the preparation of compotes and jams. True, one would have to be mad to want to return to a time of drudgery. And yet the landscape of those labors, labors eaten by doubt and carried out with heroic determination worthy of a better cause, has fused with my memories of school, and its passing also means the loss of a bitter-tasting but valuable quality, because we dealt then with imperfect objects and it was precisely their imperfection that made us concerned about them—and is not such concern often the source of an attachment similar to love? Therefore, in that distant time, an out-of-town excursion was not an escape from modern conveniences, not a playful making-difficult of existence, but, rather, the exchange of one type of work for another. Meanwhile, the old folks looked upon the technological novelties with indignation and spoke of their own youth—harder and therefore healthier—which was of course ignored.

AS ONE GOES through childhood illnesses, I went through various manias—manias more or less typical of the age or period. I collected Anglaces—flags of different countries in the chocolates of that name. Then little photographs of faraway cities, in Suchard chocolates, accumulating enough for the company to give me a stereoscope to view them. I collected stamps, but only for appearances, as I said before. Collecting for its own sake somehow never interested me. My father tried to get me to save groszy, for this purpose buying a clay piggy bank. The first I broke open, the second I plundered with the aid of a knife. After that, my father brought home a strongbox from the Savings Bank. One could put coins in it but not take them out; only the bank, where I had my own little book, could do that. This, in theory; but after examining the mechanism, I discovered that by shaking the box upside down for a very long time I could make it spit out a zloty or two, which eventually led to its complete emptying. My father gave up trying to teach me to save. And yet I was in great need of money. Nobody was giving away wires for induction coils or tinfoil for condensers and Leyden jars, or glue, or rubber bands for slingshots. And halvah, which was at the top of the list and which I needed a lot of, was quite expensive. Also cutouts. There were wonderful things then to cut out and paste, not only ordinary tanks and planes, but also gas masks that you could wear until they fell apart from saliva and breathing through the holes of the paper canister. And balloons. "Live" balloons, not the kind they have today. The ones I first got were attached to sticks, like pinwheels, the sticks in turn embedded in a raw potato to hold them. They were sold by a vendor in front of the University, but the University then was still called Parliament, perhaps out of inertia, from the Austrian time, when the building housed the Galician parliament. The little balloons came in many colors, and later had hemp strings and were filled with gas. For me there was something fascinating and at the same time sad about them. You couldn't let a balloon go; it would take off into the sky. I remember the wails of children when this happened to them in the Jesuit Garden. But a balloon wasn't happy in a house, either; it would rise to the ceiling and stay there, stubborn, stupidly and desperately butting it with its inflated head. But the next morning was worse, when I would find the balloon dying. In the course of a single night it grew wrinkled, feeble, drawn, miserable, not having enough strength now even to jump to the ceiling. It barely lifted itself above the floor, pathetically dragging its string here and there behind it. My strange partiality to balloons remained with me for many years. I bought them and hid them, afraid people would laugh at me. I pretended to fit them with gondolas, to make zeppelins out of them, but that was self-deception. I needed their brief companionship, their one-day existence, a kind of memento mori demonstrating the transience of all worldly things. There were also balloons filled with air instead of gas, on flexible copper wires, but these were dead, stillborn imitations, pretending to be what they were not, and I had nothing but contempt for them. Not taking the risk of reality, they were good only for fools. I would have nothing to do with them.

There *was* something I collected for its own sake, and persistently, for a long time: electrical-mechanical junk. To this day I have a special feeling for broken bells, alarm clocks, old radio coils, telephone speakers, and in general for objects derailed, worn out, abandoned, and which are given for the last time a chance to exist, with a pitiful vestige of respectability, at a flea market behind a theater. I went to ours often, a little like a philanthropist visiting a slum, or an animal lover secretly feeding the thinnest dogs or cats. I was a patron for old spark plugs, and bought dilapidated car magnetos, nuts, utterly useless commutators, fragments of unknown devices, and carried them home and hid them in shoe boxes, in drawers, wherever I could, even above the books on the highest shelf (I now had my own bookcase). Occasionally I would take them out and dust them off, turn a handle to make a mechanism happy, then put them carefully back. I don't know why I did this. Had someone asked me, no doubt I would have answered immediately that this thing or that might prove useful in some project—but that was not the whole truth, and I knew it.

Beyond the Eastern Fair lay what I thought was one of the most beautiful places in the world—the Amusement Park. It had carousels, a small-gauge railway, a haunted house, a fun house, and even better things. For example, a leather dummy you could punch in the mouth, with a meter that measured how hard you hit. Or a flea circus in which the little creatures were forced to pull tiny carts and carriages. Or mysterious tents—in one, when my father and I entered, an unusually broad lady undressed, not for striptease purposes but to show us the wealth of her tattoos.

My father grew uneasy when she revealed the interesting scenes on her belly, but when she went lower, I got to see only the edge of a novel landscape, because he forcibly pulled me outside. At a certain place was a stand separated from the people by a barrier. Behind the barrier—a long, low table covered with chocolates, boxes of candy. The idea was to throw a coin at these prizes; if the coin landed on a prize, it became the property of the lucky player. I quickly noticed that the larger boxes of chocolates had slightly convex lids and in addition were covered with slippery cellophane, so that the coin always slid to the table. But what are we given a brain for? At home I made a testing range out of books and pencil cases on the floor, and soon taught myself how to throw a coin so that it would land vertically and not bounce or skid. Then I calmly went to the Amusement Park. I won a big box of chocolates, but was almost immediately approached by a man with impressive shoulders who hissed into my ear, "Beat it, you little shit!" I wisely took his advice—and at home the chocolates turned out to be inedible, either moldy or rock-hard with age.

As can be seen from these little anecdotes, the years passed but some of my interests resisted the flow of time. I still loved Piasecki's halvah, and Wedel's too (in little slate boxes), moreover I discovered a candy store near the Grand Theater, the Yugoslavia, which had the best treats of the East in Lvov: Turkish delight, baklava, exotic nougats, a kvass made from bread, and many other good things. At that time, note, I weighed several kilograms more than I do today.

I spoke of the Eastern Fair. I loved to walk there when

the place was empty and no one was around. The great pavilions with dirty windows looked strange then, and my favorite spot was the big semicircle made by the longest pavilion, half of which embraced the Baczewski pavilion (the one covered with bottles of liquor). Standing under Baczewski Tower, one could awaken the echo that slept in that space; a clap of the hands, if strong enough, would be repeated four, five, even six times, and the same for a shout. A remarkably long time passed between these weaker and weaker returns of the voice, which seemed to come from an increasing distance and with an increasing effort. On cold, clear autumn days I would stand and listen to the dying throes of my echo, which held both mystery and sorrow, and though of course I knew about the principle of reflected sound waves, that had nothing to do with the special charm of the place.

It was three years before the war that I encountered for the first time, suddenly and close up, Hitlerite Germans. A red flag with a swastika appeared on one of the pavilions, and inside were many interesting machines and, on special display, tanks halfway between toys and models—faithful copies, the armor with lizard spots, the tracks, the turrets, and all the guns. The Wehrmacht emblem was proudly painted on them, in miniature, and I would soon see it again in life-size actuality, on the steel plates of the same Mark IV tanks. But at the time they were only toys, though I knew a little about the Nazis, and even then, in those toys that delighted the eye, there was something portentous, ominous, though the reduction of scale pretended innocence. The pretty tanks had a slight repugnance about them, as if they were not only and simply themselves, as if something would be hatching or growing from them. But I am not entirely sure of this. Later events may have thrown a kind of pre-storm light backward and put a tinge of evil on what was purely childlike.

CHAPTER

6

IT IS TIME now to speak about what so far I have only
hinted at: the activities—special, intense, and above all
personal—to which I devoted myself both in school and at
home. That I could accomplish so much (and the amount
of that labor will become evident in a moment) astonishes
me today, when there is usually not time enough for anything. Time evidently is more stretchable when we are
young, and with appropriately focused effort it can be expanded to make additional room, like the pockets of my
school uniform, in which (in keeping with tradition) I

carried more than their prosaic dimensions allowed. Or can it be that space itself favors children? Surely that is impossible, and yet my pockets held rolls of string (for sailor's knots and emergencies), a collection of favorite screws, a penknife, erasers that disappeared (did I eat them?), a small brass chain from a toilet, spools, rubber bands, a protractor, a small compass (not so much for geometrical purposes as to be used against fat Z., who sat in front of me), a vial filled with crushed match heads (a poison, also an explosive), a magnifying glass turned cloudy from scratches, an exhausted wallet, various treasures provided by nature according to the season (acorns, chestnuts), half a yo-yo (useless but somehow valuable), a small puzzle with movable squares, called the Fifteen, another puzzle with three pigs (a game of dexterity, under a round glass), not to mention the entire contents of my desk, which I took with me from home to school and from school to home. This—and I don't know how or when I got the original idea—was for making identification papers.

I worked during class, under the pretense of taking notes, behind my open notebook raised a little with my left hand—worked calmly, on a large scale, and solely for myself, showing nothing of it to anyone. I skip over my period of apprenticeship and proceed to the mastery I achieved in my second and third years at the gymnasium. First I would cut small sheets of paper from a notebook—the paper. had to be glossy—and these were folded in two to make a booklet, which I bound using a special method. The number 560 on our school badges was made of tiny spirals of hair-thin silver thread, and that is what I sewed the spine with. After accumulating a number of booklets of different sizes, which was important, I gave them covers made of the finest materials: bristol, drawing paper, and I encased certain special booklets in high-quality cardboard cut from the covers of class exercise books. When the recess bell rang, I hid all this in my bag, and in the next class began the slow, precise work of filling the empty pages. I used ink, India ink, colored pencils, and coins pressed as stamps in the appropriate places.

What kind of identity papers were these? All kinds—conferring authority over a certain territory, with limitations, and documents of empowerment, and titles, and licenses and warrants, and on the longer pages I hand-printed various checks and payable-to-bearer certificates for kilograms of ore, usually platinum and gold, and vouchers for precious gems. I made passports for emperors and monarchs, assigned to them dignitaries, chancellors, each of whom could produce papers at a moment's notice, and I fashioned meticulous coats of arms and produced special passes with validations and authorizations, and since I had plenty of time, this legitimizing seemed to have no end. I began bringing to school old postage stamps, which I modified to make seals, creating a hierarchy of them, from the little triangulars through the rectangulars to the highest—top-secret, perfect circles with mystic signs in the middle that would make anyone fall to his knees. Developing a taste for this labor, I issued permits for the collecting of diamonds as big as human heads, and to the permits I appended riders, and to the riders, codicils, rising ever higher in the realm of power and authority, until the only valid documents were in code and protected by a system of exacting passwords and symbols. Certain papers even had their own decoding booklets, their meaning was so awe-some; without the booklets they were only numbered pages covered with incomprehensible calligraphy.

I read a story somewhere at that time, and it made a great impression on me. It was a tale about an expedition into the heart of Africa. The explorers, crossing mountains and jungles, encountered an unknown tribe of savages who knew a terrible word, to be uttered only in extremis, for whoever heard it turned into a mound of jelly about a meter high. The mounds were described in detail, also the simple stratagem used by the savages so they would not turn into jelly themselves: when screaming the transmuting word, they put their fingers in their ears. I remembered this dreadful word, and did not have the courage at first to say it out loud, impressed by the fate of one scientist, an unbeliever, who laughed at the account given by the only surviving member of the expedition, and shouted it—with tragic, gelatinous consequences. The word capable of changing a man into an aspic was *ämälän*.

Considering this story from the vantage point of today, I wonder if the author's intention was not humorous. If so, the humor failed to reach me. To be sure, I did not believe the story was true; yet it left me with the uneasy feeling that there were words that could somehow cause fatal re-sults. I reasoned: If certain sounds could put a person into a hypnotic trance, why couldn't some special combination of sounds have an even stronger effect, not through magic but through the influence of waves acting in the air on the ear . . . and so on.

Ämälän clearly needed to be incorporated into the sphere of authorization, where I had now become an expert. It inspired many passwords. Since I was not a bad student, no one looked into my book bag, books, or notebooks—a good thing, because dozens of tiny booklets would have been discovered, some filled with writing, some blank, and there were experimental samples, too, in which I tried, unfortunately without success, to increase the eloquence of the documents with watermarks. My lust for realistic detail was not satisfied in that case, despite innumerable attempts.

I was building a kingdom of universal permission, universal power, but such defining words did not appear in the course of my creative effort. Following my bureaucratic instinct, I rightly mistrusted transcendent ideas, sticking to the system of centimeters–grams–seconds, that is, I always specified in respectable units of measurement what the bearer could do. As for the blank booklets, each had a serial number, certifying signatures, and notarizing seals placed at the very bottom, so they wouldn't be invalidated by a paper blemish or an error in positioning. Naturally all the blank pages also had a perforated line so they could be torn from the booklet and presented. After much trial and error I accomplished this with a small toothed wheel taken from an alarm clock and always kept in my pencil case, which also contained one of my father's razor blades, for cutting pages. More than once I accidentally cut into my desk as well, but somehow it wasn't noticed.

It may seem strange that I never showed my friends these invoices for sacks of rubies and deeds to empires overseas. But my friends might have laughed, and this was no laughing matter to me. What I probably felt—without knowing it—was the fear and shame of an artist asked to explain his work in no-nonsense terms: What exactly is this and what purpose does it serve? To have answered that it was only for amusement would have been a lie, at least partly, because more was involved. What more? To this day I don't know, but I was right nevertheless. People nowadays complain about the general decline of art, the lack of ideas, the shallowness, frivolous experimentation, ephemeral fashion. We feel this particularly in the presence of the continuing power of works of the past, the cathedrals of Florence and Siena, the mysteries of ancient Chinese theater, the African gods cured with smoke. We leave an exhibit of Paleolithic art or the Sistine Chapel and wonder what happened to the human spirit, why it lost its capacity to focus, erupt, command like an elemental force, compelling acceptance as trees do, clouds, the bodies of animals and men. They tell us that artists have ceased to be a lightning rod that catches and accumulates energy from above. They tell us that art has been killed by the possibility of unlimited choice, the knowledge that conventions are but conventions—he who knows it is possible to write or paint in any style and on any subject will produce nothing great. In his freedom he finds the grave of his talent.

Consider the photograph of astronauts leaving their ship in outer space. How unsuited is the human body for infinity, how helpless it becomes, showing its absurdity with every movement, bereft of the saving limits and justifying resistance of ground, walls, ceiling. It is no accident that the astronaut assumes the position of a fetus in the womb, bowing the head, bending the knees, keeping the arms close to the body; it is no accident that the tether connecting him to the ship resembles an umbilical cord. We are buoyant, energetic, full of direction and purpose only in the prison of gravity; it is in gravity's thrall only that our body finds its sense, and every joint and nerve has use and therefore beauty. Natural purpose, inevitability, the feeling that we are in the presence of the only possible solution to a problem—this is what every great work of art evokes. The Lord God of Michelangelo, with thick curly beard, folds of robe, and bare feet with veins showing, did not come from the free play of the artist's mind. The painter had to work in obedience to the literature of absolute dictates going back to Genesis. A Michelangelo of today— his soul made irresolute by skepticism, that great stink of knowledge—at every step encounters paradoxes, dilemmas, absurdities, of which the Renaissance master never dreamed. The toenails of the Lord God are short. If He has a body like a man's, those nails should grow. And since He endures eternally, they should have grown into snaking horns that go from naked toes to all the galaxies, filling the sky with sweeping spirals of keratin. Could one, should one paint such a thing? And if not, we are faced with the problem of the Divine pedicure. The nails are short either by cutting or miracle—surely one who can stop the sun in its path can stop the growth of a toenail. Both solutions are unacceptable: the first smacks of barbershop, the second of blasphemy. No, the toenails must be short without disquisition or analysis.

Here we have an imposed limitation that makes art possible, for art answers the potentially endless series of questions with an act of faith. The rigor of liturgy must of course be internalized, the burning hair shirt put on voluntarily, the barrier embraced by an ardent heart rather than enforced by the police. There are spiritual barriers and police barriers, and if the latter do not inspire great works, it is only because the policeman controls others and is not the functionary of his own art, a worshiper of its rules and regulations. The command must come from above, the limit must be given by revelation—and accepted without questions about proof or purpose, just as we do not question the leaves, stars, or sand beneath our feet. Faith takes on a reality that is completely inflexible, absolute; while the spirit—only in such chains, obedient, yet in its obedience attempting to express the world and itself—creates in the greatest freedom. This applies to all forms of art marked by a great seriousness that rules out irony, distance, humor—for how can one make light of gravel, a bird's wing, the motions of the sun and moon? Or take dance—its freedom is an illusion, the dancer submitting to the tyranny of the music, which governs his every movement, and individual expression lies only in the narrowest margin of interpretation.

True, there can be sublime limits outside religion, but then they have to be given sacred status; one must believe they are inevitable and not invented. The knowledge that something could be completely otherwise, the rejection of inevitability in favor of an ocean of conscious techniques, styles, devices, shackles the mind and hands with the freedom of choice. The artist, like the astronaut in weightless space, turns helplessly, with nothing to grab hold of.

In that early, bureaucratic phase of my creativity, I came close indeed to the sacred wellspring of art. What the celestial Thrones, Dominions, and Seraphim were for Michelangelo, documented authorization was for me. One would be greatly mistaken to think that I was letting my imagination run wild. I was a willing slave of the liturgy of officialdom, a petty bureaucrat of Genesis, a chubby schoolboy transformed into a lowly clerk of the Decalogue brought up to date by the administrative grace of Red Tape. Today, in the gloomier, self-conscious stage of creativity, I would no doubt take this theme to the comic absurd, issuing licenses for galaxies to move and proofs of age for geological epochs. But back then, as Michelangelo did not worry about toenails, I never asked by what right the Law issued birth certificates to newborns, for in my innocence I equated legal documentation with the Absolute— and thus stood on the threshold of art. Minding letter and seal and making sure the blank forms were in order and the signatures correct, I was in preordained harmony with authorization orthodoxy, to which all doubts and hesitations and indeterminacy were completely foreign.

My first steps were small, uncertain, but taken in the right direction. I never overreached my authority, despite the fact that, or perhaps because, I did not know Whose instrument I was. Therefore I did not fill in the names on the identity papers of kings and prime ministers; I left empty places also for their photographs and signatures, and kept those documents, marked "At the Request of Bearer," in a special compartment of my book bag that was closed with two buttons, to make sure they did not fall into the wrong hands. In matters dealing with the treasury I was especially careful to nip in the bud any possibility of fraud or embezzlement. I specified the sums, quantities, purchasing power of the coins at my disposal, and from the uncertain value of generalized gold switched to bricks, bars, ingots (my vouchers gave a precise description of the ingot, which I standardized, using my physics textbook; my model was the platinum-iridium bar kept in Sèvres, near Paris, which served as the measure of one meter), and I even gave the dimensions for nuggets, as described in the books of Karl May and Jack London, to be paid in leather bags tied with a lasso cut into suitable pieces. Obtaining the necessary information from Professor Wyrobek's *Marvels of Nature*, I permitted the disbursement of rubies, spinels, chalcedonies, chrysoprases, malachites, and opals, listing on detachable stubs the grade of the gem, the cut, the carats, the number ordered, and I also made booklets of special bonus coupons—which led to a problem. Was it proper, for example, to give someone, say, a platinum dish through official channels? My bureaucratic instinct said no, that words like "give" or "gift" were inappropriate. "Disburse," "allocate," "deliver" were all right. Also, with a gold chain, the worst someone could do was wear it, whereas a dish, even of platinum, someone could actually eat off it—a prospect offensive to a clerk's cut-and-dried mind. Oh, it was not lust for material things that moved me to shower pearls and rain emeralds (but counted to the drop); payment for services rendered was simply an inescapable part of the world I had created. And I issued special passes, also according to a hierarchy—for the Outer Gate, the Middle Gate, the First, Second, and Third Doors—with stubs to be torn off by guards. The interior halls and passageways were heavily guarded, and their names were known to the lower echelons; the next, more interior, were known only by code; and slowly a shape began to emerge from nothingness, a Building, a Castle unbelievably High, with a

Center of Mystery never named, not even by the most daring—the place where, after passing through all the gates, halls, and guard stations, you could finally receive full authorization!

It is easy to describe now, but how very far I was from the Center then, inching my way as a conscientious and humble scribe, medieval calligrapher, patient as an ant over my uppercase and lowercase letters, not knowing how or when my incunabula would cross the line from booklet to Book, or how or when the scribbler would become a writer, the copyist an artist!

Acquiring a certain proficiency, even using red ink to make the Bureau more versatile, I wisely remained conservative as to content. I was not prodigal in the dispensing of kingdoms, nor did I allow, in any one kingdom, too much power to accrue to any one individual. It would have been easy to have a universal passport that opened every door of the Castle and every treasury vault. But—and let it be recorded to my credit—I never drew up such a document. I remember a booklet I prepared for an inspector extraordinary and plenipotentiary. Each page, colored with a different crayon, added to his powers. I could see him presenting the first page, no doubt to lower functionaries, an ordinary page with only two triangular seals. The gatekeepers reluctantly slide back the bolts. Then, turning slightly, he produces the second page, green, and now officers, seeing it, stiffen. And then onto the table in the guardhouse are thrown the third and fourth pages, dazzling white, with the round Great Seal, blood-red, and they stand at attention, trembling, and salute as he proceeds to the Main Door, where the Gatekeeper-General, who a moment before was inaccessibility personified, in a uniform fairly dripping with gold, now is all asweat with official zeal, and the sound of the lock opening blends with the tinkling of the medals on his chest, and the old man is a statue at attention, his gleaming sword aloft—honoring not the person who crosses the threshold but the paper the Emissary casually holds in his hand. How delicious, the thought of that wonderful dealing out of safe-conducts, those increasing doses of Perfectly Legal Power! No battle scene out of Sienkiewicz, no thunder of cannon could ever match the rustle of the Coupons of Power settling on the gray table within the gray walls of the Castle! The magic hidden in the Great Seal—even I could not fathom it, for in the center lay a Sign Secret Unto Itself, that is, a Code Without a Key, which meant that the bearer must be an Emissary of the Unnameable!

Was he, then, an inspector sent by the Creator, an executor of the Lord God Himself? I do not know. He came out of nowhere and, having done his duty, would return to nowhere.

Did I actually imagine all this so artistically and precisely? Yes and no. By giving authorizations, I also accepted their authority; thus between myself and them arose ties and tensions that in turn pointed the way for me to follow. I made up no stories, constructed no plots; they came into being themselves, peopling the empty spaces in particular documents. The papers were what drove the complex drama of the Bureau; they were the sun around which moved, like planets, the thrones, guards, minions. Thus I had to be always present, in every place and at every moment, to supply in an emergency the proper form, without which the matter at hand—its country, its world—would shrivel, fade, and die. Bureaucracy didn't merely punctuate the action; it created it.

Consider how modern was this gymnasium discovery of mine. Ignorant of the rules of writing, I strengthened the setting, the atmosphere, not describing any person or scene directly. Everything placed in the drama of the Bureau was placed only by implication, extrapolation: from particular documents one could make inferences about the lives existing beyond them, just as one inferred, from a branching shadow, the existence of a tree, the sun, and the laws of optics. The antinovel of the second half of the twentieth century focused solely on objects, but my universal asceticism went further than the antinovel, because I wrote—exercising the ultimate self-restraint—only blank forms! Doing this, I jettisoned the old-fashioned background of landscape or cityscape, and the psychology of characterization, and the traditional twists and complications of plot, and all the verbal formulas of literature, the tired tricks of clauses, modifiers, adverbs. I used no structures, new or old, no archetypes, quoted no cogent thought or pungent saying, sticking to my stamps, drawing pen, and toothed wheel, with them getting to the heart of the matter every time—because it was through such total literary abstinence that I proved that an entire world could be expressed by silence!

My bureaucratic imagination was such, that these papers could not be arranged along a single time line, since certain periods (dynastic, for example) had multiple versions, sometimes parallel, sometimes tangled, and others were like archipelagoes in many dimensions. During math and Latin classes, when the rigor of their discipline made it impossible for me to do any work, I would pretend to listen but in my mind review the authorizations to be issued that day, slowly savoring the kaleidoscope they made, set in alternating rows along which I could build an endless number of variations for any sequence of events.

But didn't I become lost in this vastness? After all, I kept no files, following only the voice of red tape in my ear. I knew no path through the paper labyrinth, but the point was to wander with panache. Errors that occur once are merely clerical, unimportant, a speck on the photograph of Existence, a tiny blemish on a faithful reproduction. But a whole edifice of error, appropriately complex, can become a dwelling for the soul, a seat of autonomous meanings, a structure less and less dependent on prototypes, a version of things liberated from the dictates of naturalism—in short, a New and Opposing Edition of Reality. The culmination of error is, of course, a philosophical system, that is, a proposition of values for which it is worth living and dying. This is the road upward, where misunderstanding becomes revelation, a pompous lie an epic, violence done to logic poetry, and the obstinate persistence in error the greatest fidelity of which man is capable.

I believe my paper odyssey in gymnasium met these conditions. I drew up documents that were so stupid, their stupidity grew into perversion (as when I gave the conspirators of a palace coup authorization to commit regicide). Leaving behind all common sense, they acquired a lyrical sense, for I mixed dynasties and shuffled torture chambers, treasuries, staffs, and regulations, breaking the shackles of time and space, making document contradict document, putting paragraphs at loggerheads, canceling coronations, reversing births and executions; I was so careless, I committed *Crimen Laese Legitimationis*, opening the door even to apocalyptic expectations. True, such confusion was produced only by the abstracted, inattentive hand that held the seal, but an alert subject-recipient could have not only straightened out that mess but also given it a different, diabolical interpretation: saying that these were not accidental lapses but the seismic effects of secret battles, that even within the Bureau itself there was not complete agreement, that antagonistic factions there were locked in cruel struggle, that certain offices were treacherously trying to undermine others, and that even the highest of the high did not have full control over the Great Seal, because the lower levels wrestled with them fiercely, constantly, and this silent bureaucratic wrestling was in its hopeless irrevocability like the eternal revolving of worlds in space. And because I not only made errors but repeated myself often, two very modern spirits assisted in my creation: Obscurity and Boredom.

But how can I expect—someone asks—such interpretive willingness to be bestowed on a fat schoolboy's scribbling? Isn't the joke a bit overstretched? My answer: In art, we too timidly pass over in silence the absolute necessity of an audience's willingness to interpret. We teach and are taught that a work of art is like a rake lying in the dark. One who steps on it gets hit in the head, is dazzled with sudden light, and it is the same with a brilliant work: the viewer is struck with sudden, unexpected bliss. This noble lie is so deeply rooted that when, a few years after the time described here, I had to flee the Gestapo from an apartment that had been "blown," leaving behind, among my belongings, a note-book of poems in longhand, I felt regret at the loss sustained by our nation's culture but was also convinced that those of my pursuers who knew Polish would be aesthetically bowled over. Later, a little wiser, I blushed at this memory, but only because I realized how awful my sonnets had been—still not understanding that the quality of the poetry was completely irrelevant in that situation. This world of ours would look very different if Gestapo hearts could be influenced by verse. Art compels no one; we are transported by it only if we consent to be transported. Therefore the element of mutual cheering in this, the praise purchasing praise, the tit-for-tat endorsement, and therefore the fraud and collective prevarication—Gombrowicz opened our eyes to that.

But there is more to it, and on a higher level: more to the talent of reading. Any child can read the virtuous tale of Cinderella, but, without sophistication and Freud, how will you see it as a ballet of perversion created by a sadist for masochists? Nowadays to deny that obscenity lies concealed in fairy tales only shows your naiveté. Next you will say that the detective in Robbe-Grillet's *Erasers* was a bungler, for that is the work's literal text, and that Hamlet's inconsistent behavior came from Shakespeare's incorporating into the play too many different elements from previous versions. The modern scientist points to the sky, where the stars are scattered randomly, and yet everyone knows that they form the zodiac shapes of gods, animals, and people. For in general we can ennoble a work or call it shallow, depending on the backdrop we give it on the stage of our mind as we read. Nor is it a passive backdrop, but a system of references, where a broken stick may suggest a stylized branch of ancient Japan, and a notched stone a sculpture expressing the mood of our fragmented time. Thus, coming upon an error, one could cry, "Inconsistency!" or, conversely, "Brilliant dissonance!" or, "The abyss, depicted by the intentional cracking of the shell of logic!" Of course not everyone can affix an entirely new referential backdrop to a work of art; there are experts for that, who themselves are often at a loss—which gives rise to debates, feuds, and conferences. And the artists don't help, becoming less explicit and more cryptic about their work to make it semantically richer. Admittedly, town hall meetings and councils of elders will not be very impressed with the creative efforts of a gymnasium student, but if we know the mechanism of a phenomenon, and the phenomenon is the same, we can at least ask for equal treatment—and not merely in our own interest, for we do suspect that in the depths of dusty libraries lie many undiscovered Musils and Canettis, many works that will never awake to eminence if we do not help them by presenting their case.

But at the age of twelve I did not know all this. Scrupulous about limiting power, even sovereign power, and remaining anonymous in my antlike toil, I disappeared in the work I created, never went to extremes, never permitted paper inflation, and thanks to this constant modesty was able to join sacred and realistic. Sacred, because I took as my axiom that in the Beginning was Authorization; realistic, because my activity was suggested by the Spirit of the Time itself. And if I was ever beckoned by an Almighty License, a Document of Documents heavy with seals like red wax suns and with garlands of multicolored cords, conceived in the *Summis Auspicis* of Chaos, where clauses and files still swirled in a state free of the Office Ladder (which in another context became the Ladder to Heaven), I put that temptation from me, that sacrilege, the greedy desire to get to the Heart all at once, as if I sensed that that would be futile, the attempt doomed to failure. It was only through the closest attention to detail—the invoice for a hundred sacks of coarse gold sand payable to bearer (but only of the Fifth Order), the booklet sewn with silver thread for the Executioner, Category II—it was only by joining Being and Obligation on my desk, under cover of a textbook, that I was able to raise bureaucracy, by its nature a lifeless and sterile thing, to the level of art. On wings of authorization I soared above the gray vale of tears, and as I flew I plucked from nonexistence whole worlds with the stroke of a pen and the touch of a cogged wheel from an alarm clock. Not even thirteen, I wedded literature and graphics (both necessary for making documents) to create a new movement. Authorizationism—that is, sacrobureaucratic art under the double patronage, metaphysical, allusional, of Saint Peter and the Policeman in one person, because authorizing documents are made, after all, to be shown to someone.

Not that I believed my work—surely it was only a game I played during history class, geography, and even, oh shame, Polish, and yet . . . I never showed those papers of mine to anybody, and such was my state of mind that, had I found on the street an authorization to dig up treasure on Sand Mountain, I would have been overjoyed—but not surprised. . . . Because, and this is difficult for me to express, although I knew I was not producing True Documents, at the same time I felt that, nevertheless, some flicker of truth lay in them. That this was not all nonsense, though at the same time it was—but nonsense only literally. I was well aware that no one would honor my vouchers for pails of rubies, that they were not worth a grosz, but if I had not created that kind of value, perhaps I had created another. What kind? A value that was intrinsic, like the cathedrals of Orvieto and Siena, which an atheist attempts to diminish, to dismiss, saying they are very large buildings with black and white stripes like pajamas. It was much easier, of course, to laugh at *my* cathedral, which was not even material, which existed not as a thing but as a metaphor— or, as a modern cyberneticist might put it, as an analog model of multivalent relations, of polysemy. Feeling that no one would understand what I myself couldn't put into words, that only my infantilism would be seen, I kept silent and preserved the secret.

The work of that period has unfortunately been lost, including the most valuable, the decree in the matter of Physical Education, stamped with a two-groszy coin (of the rare series of Lesser Seals) and reinforced by a piece of yellow shoelace during recess. Also lost, the permit to Imprison Suspects, printed in Red Cipher with passwords using the Secret Key, First Class (my knowledge of codes derived mainly from *The Adventures of the Good Soldier Schweik*). The works were lost, but the path remained, pointing, promising.

Since I did all this office work only at the gymnasium (at home I did not have the patience to sit, whereas in class I had to), at home I was free to read, and read a great deal. I read Buyno-Arctowa's *Isle of Sages*, which was a kind of premonition of science fiction. Overworked as I was, and therefore absentminded, I served as treasurer in the student government and could never balance the account, so my father had to bail me out with a zloty or two each month. Not that I was embezzling public funds—it was simply that groszy dues would get mixed up in my head with the sacks of gold and diamonds I was disbursing, and that confusion led to deficits.

Observing office hours like a professional bureaucrat, at home I would not even glance at my authorizations. Between the tutor, the Frenchwoman, and supper, I occupied myself with a completely different form of creativity: inventions. In school, preoccupied with the Bureau, I gave no thought to them, while at home, as at the turn of a switch, all my thoughts moved in another direction. This did not trouble me. I would have been hard put to say which of the two activities I regarded as more important. I was like a man with two wives who, sincere and devoted to each in turn, knows how to divide himself between them, for everything has been arranged perfectly.

Going home, I knew where to buy wire, glue, paraffin, screws, sandpaper, and when my allowance wasn't enough, I would either touch my uncle—my mother's brother and a physician like my father—or concoct some scheme. This uncle—I called him by his first name, almost as if he were a schoolmate—had occasional fits of generosity, which didn't please my parents. I often got a five-zloty piece from him, with Pilsudski on it; I didn't put it in my horseshoe change purse but held it, to be safe, in my fist. I remember walking through the city with the sweaty coin in my hand and feeling like Harun al-Rashid incognito. My eye, falling on the store windows, would instantly turn that piece of silver into a hundred things on display; but, suddenly as hard and miserly as a millionaire, I did not deign to do them the favor of a purchase. I generally invested my wealth in inventions, and found out that all real inventors do this, that inventions can consume a great sum of money without a trace—and without results.

As a bureaucrat I was tranquil, because passionate bureaucracy is impossible; as an inventor I was not tranquil. The sacred flame of technology blazed hot within me. I made bloody sacrifices to it, from constantly bleeding, bandaged fingers, and was stubborn in defeat, brokenhearted yet always reviving with new ideas, new hope. For a long time I worked on an electric motor that resembled Watt's steam engine, but instead of a piston and flywheel it had a coil whose magnetic field sucked in an iron rod. A special circuit breaker sent current into the winding. I later learned that this device had already been invented and that such motors existed, or, rather, used to exist, for they were inefficient and too slow. But that didn't matter. This was the first time, I think, I showed my extraordinary tenacity, because I built and rebuilt that prototype maybe fifty times before it finally moved. And when it moved, an awkward thing of twisted metal scrounged from a tinsmith who had his shop in our building, amid a confusion of wires, oil stains, dead batteries, junk, hammers and pliers (the blood of massacred toys still on them), I sat and watched the creaking, slow, jerky rotations, the hesitating levers, the little sparks at the circuit breaker. I watched, dirty, weary, and triumphant. If I boasted later, demonstrating the motor to the household, I did only what any boy my age would have done. But the important thing was that moment when it was accomplished, the creative act realized, and there was nothing more for me to do: the motor went, limping, until dusk, and I watched. A very special kind of satisfaction it was, requiring no praise from others, and not even witnesses. I needed no one, because it had come to pass. Watt and Stephenson could not have experienced a greater happiness.

Of course, this feat did not suffice; I thirsted for new victories. For a long time I worked on electrolysis, dropping all sorts of substances into water, and not in the expectation that gold would someday appear on the electrodes. I was not interested in gold but in the creation of a substance that did not exist. I scraped brown, rust-red, and gray powders from the electrodes and carefully put them in boxes. Concluding finally that my data were insufficient, I returned to electrical apparatuses, this time more systematically, using a thick German book with Gothic print, *Elektronisches Experimentierbuch*. I had taken two years of German in gymnasium but couldn't read the language—that is, couldn't understand it, not a single sentence. So I had to tackle the text with a dictionary, a little like Champollion and Egyptian hieroglyphics. It was slow going but produced results, because I finally read that book cover to cover and built a Wimshurst machine and a Ruhmkorff coil—for some reason I loved powerful electrical discharges. I was by nature slovenly, extremely impatient, and careless, which makes it all the more surprising that I was capable of so much self-discipline and mulish repetition in the face of discouragement. Twice I went through several months of murderous toil and cut fingers and bruised knuckles and dirty bandages, wrapping several kilometers of inductor wire onto small paper bobbins that I'd glued, covering each layer with paraffin, putting wax paper in between, and it was worse with the electrostatic machine, because I couldn't get the right material for its disks. First I tried old gramophone records from a motion-picture theater, one-sided and with a diameter of maybe sixty centimeters, but they turned out to be worthless. Finally I obtained some plates from a very old and broken Wimshurst machine. With a fretsaw I cut these down to smaller plates, discarding the ebonite at the edges, which was green with age, and turned them on a lathe, in a foul cloud of black dust that got into my hair, eyes, teeth, fingernails. At last the machine was built. It is funny that at the same time I was never good with my hands; whatever I made in shop at school was crooked, wobbly, not properly finished, and got a poor grade.

Next I constructed a Tesla transformer, and delighted in the unearthly glow of the Geissler tubes in a high-voltage field. At that time the little store in Hausmann's Alley that sold scientific supplies became the place I besieged. I remember that a Wimshurst machine, small but much better than mine, cost ninety zlotys, the price of a suit. Years later, in my first year at medical school, the first money I ever received in my life—a stipend for the Medical Institute (this was 1940)—I blew entirely on Geissler tubes. My Wimshurst machine was still working. It disappeared only after the outbreak of war in 1941.

I was a theorist, too, having a pile of notebooks in which I recorded my inventions, with "blueprints." I remember some of them. There was a device for cutting corn kernels in such a way that the cooked hulls remained on the cob; an airplane shaped like a parabolic mirror so that, flying above the clouds, it could collect the sun's rays and convert them to steam that drove a turbine that drove a propeller; a bicycle without pedals, which you rode like a horse, the seat acting as a piston that turned a toothed pivot that turned the wheels. Another kind of bicycle had a front-wheel drive, where the handlebars were pumped like bellows and connected by rods to a camshaft, as in a locomotive. And a car that used cigarette-lighter flints for spark plugs. And an electromagnetic cannon—I actually built a small model, only to learn that someone had thought of that long before me. And an oar in the shape of an umbrella, which under the influence of the resistance of the water alternately opened and closed. My greatest invention was the sun-and-planet gear—like many of my inventions, unoriginal—I didn't even know its name—but at least the thing was real and is used even today. And of course there were perpetual-motion machines—I thought up a dozen of those. I had notebooks devoted entirely to automobiles. One idea, for example, was to have a small three-cylinder engine, like those in planes, set in each wheel. (A variant of that was actually used, but with electric motors.) I also recall an idea for a two-piston engine, and even a kind of rocket propelled by rhythmic bursts in its combustion chamber. I thought about my rocket when I read—in 1944, or maybe 1945—of the German V-1. Obviously I'm not claiming to have invented the V-1 before the Germans, but the principle was similar.

In addition I designed various machines of war: a one-man tank, a flat steel coffin on tracks with a machine gun and a motorcycle engine; a tank-missile; tanks that moved on the principle of a screw instead of treads; planes able to take off vertically. And a great many other machines, big and small, filled my black notebooks as well as the notebooks with marbled covers. I could draw well enough, but my specifications were imaginary and all the numbers and details made up.

Meanwhile my library was growing, abundant now in popular-science books, various Marvels of Nature and Secrets of the Universe. Other notebooks were filling up, these with designs not of machines but of animals, for I had taken over the reins of Evolution, serving as Chief Constructor. I developed terrible predators based on dinosaurs, creatures with shields and horns and serrated teeth, and for the longest time I tried to make an animal that had a wheel instead of legs. I went about it rigorously, beginning with a drawing of its skeleton, adapting bone and tendon to elements taken from a locomotive.

Describing at length my engineering efforts, in the lower gymnasium, to discover Americas already discovered, and telling of the great toil this involved, I do not forget that it was all, after all, a game. I set obstacles for myself, I measured my strength against my goals, which sometimes were set too high, because I also suffered defeats—for example, when I tried to imitate Edison and build a phonograph. I used every kind of needle, diaphragm, rolling pin, wax, paraffin, foil, and though I screamed myself hoarse into the horn of one phonograph after another, I never got a machine to respond with even the weakest squeak of a recorded voice. But, I repeat, it was a game. I knew this at the age of twelve, and today I agree with that twelve-year-

old, though with a few reservations. That destructive period in my life, when I would take apart whatever fell into
my hands, did not pass into the next, constructive, period
overnight; there was a transition, and that transition, it
seems to me now, is more interesting as a phenomenon
than either: a period of pretend work. In other words, for
quite a while—before my great feats of engineering—I
built radio apparatuses, receivers and transmitters, that
could not function, nor were they meant to function. Put
together from old spools of thread and burned-out tubes
and condensers and thick copper wire, provided with a
great number of impressive knobs and gauges mounted on
little boards and set in empty tea tins—realistic copies of
real radios—if they did not satisfy me, did not look serious
enough, I would add to their importance by inserting into
that artful tangle a shiny piece of tin here, a specially
twisted spring there, until some instinct said that this was
enough, the pseudoradio had come up to my expectations.
It was a game. I was playing. Yet it is curious, the similarity
between those constructions and the things you find today
in art exhibits. Was I ahead of my time in art as well? Too
flattering a thought, especially as I recall a recent experience I had at a show of abstract sculpture.

The center of the exhibition was occupied by squat
pretzel-like antitorsos and antinudes; and collages (why not
simply call them cutouts?) of various types and materials
hung on the walls. I passed completely empty canvases on
easels, canvases poked from behind in a few places by pegs,
so that the sheetlike surfaces were broken into geometric
shapes, and I passed gray-brown-green sackcloth forms in
frames, forms whose material the eye could recognize only

very close up—shreds of netting stuck under mastic or glue, iron fillings, rubber shells—but at the next work I stopped. A quiet thing, as if the artist had decided to choose the strategy of restraint: it had a rectangular frame made of metal. About two-fifths up from the bottom edge—the proportion of the "golden section"—was a carelessly attached bar emphasizing the position, and above that line stretched a barren field of metal old to the point of senility, with three nearly equidistant holes at the center. The holes, drilled through, gaped into space, each surrounded by a dark gray halo. Blinded stars, suns like eyes put out! I wondered what technique the artist had used to dust those openings so naturally with a pale ash that slowly blended into nothingness, and I marveled at the skill with which he had annealed the metal surface, for it was fused-smooth yet at the same time bubbled-lumpy in places, as if from flame. I looked for the card with the work's title and the artist's name, but there was none. Then, blinking, I realized my mistake. The exhibit was in a large, beautifully vaulted cellar, the artwork hung on unplastered walls, and here and there, as is common in cellars, in recesses in the brick were the registers of furnace ducts. I was standing in front of one of these, a rusty vent with a twisted damper bar. Instantly the aesthetic light emanating from that register to my eager eyes dimmed and was extinguished; the thing, unmasked, humbled, became a banal piece of metal over a flue, and I moved away hurriedly, embarrassed, to return to the exhibit and put myself again in the frame of mind appropriate for meeting the challenge of abstract art.

Thinking about this adventure, I concluded that there was no reason to be ashamed. If anyone was to blame for that easy misunderstanding, it was not I. I recall how a certain expert—a true art lover, though admittedly somewhat nearsighted—at another exhibit stepped past a multitude of lumps and lobes in stone gray and plaster-of-Paris white, and proceeded quickly to a piece on a base right at the entrance. He was drawn by its unusual color. It was a small, roundish piece with surfaces woven rhythmically. He froze in mid-stride, winced, and slowly turned away, because it was an ordinary challah, the creation of only a baker. The woman operating the cash register had set it there while she went out for tea.

What is going on with art, that it allows the possibility of such amusing substitutions? Can it be that the role of purveyor of its fashionable products is playable also by a chimney sweep, a baker, a fantasizing child? The answer is not that simple. In the past an artist produced things that were necessary socially; they were instruments, albeit of a special kind, that helped the dead to reach eternity, spells to be cast, prayers to be liturgically fleshed, the barren woman to conceive, the hero to receive sacral distinction. The aesthetic component of those instruments enhanced their function but was never central, never an independent, nonutilitarian thing. An artist thus had a definite place in the transcendental edifices of religion and government. He was the engineer-performer of a theme, not its author, for authorship was attributed to Revelation, to the Absolute. Hence the strict limits we have spoken of so much; hence also the tautological nature of ancient art, which never says anything new but repeats by heart what is well known: Crucifixion, Annunciation, Assumption, the act of procreation in priapic symbols, the struggle between Ormazd and Ahriman. As for his personality, his unique genius, the artist smuggled that, as it were, deep in the canvas or sculpture or altar, and the greater the talent, the greater the ingenuity in manifesting itself despite the need to submit to the liturgical recipe and remain in the narrow margin of the permitted. Because the artist was able to move the frozen dogma a little, to set it vibrating, to give it a resonance that more or less reflected the contemporary real world; he was also able, conversely, to conceal himself in the work through dissonances, discords barely perceptible—whose interpretation today may be altogether wrong, since what to us is naive or even comical in the figures of early Gothic saints, for example, may not have been at all naive or comical for the people living then. I would love to have seen the face of one of those artists when he was alone with his saint taking shape. The smuggling of one's personality into a metaphysical dogma fascinates me, because in many masterpieces I sense the active presence of the creator—a kind of unconscious sabotage or microscopic blasphemy, whose drop of poison paradoxically strengthens the official, holy message. But that era has passed, the house of metaphysical bondage has fallen under the nudges of technology, and the artist now finds himself terribly free. Instead of a decalogue of themes, an infinite world; instead of revelation, a search; instead of commands, a choice. We have evolution: the literal nude, the nude rough-hewn, a stone generalization of the body, a geometrical hint of the body, a fragment, a piece chopped off, a ruined torso or head, and finally someone in a dry riverbed selects a rock out of a million around it, because of its particular shape, and carries it to an art exhibit. And so one goes, *nolens volens*, from fate as Omniscient Providence to fate as the theory of statistics—a blind boil of forces carving rocks in the current of a river. From a Conscious Creator to creative randomness. From Necessity to Chance.

It is not only the artist who suffers from too much freedom; the public is no better off. The game, then, is of creative attempts and thumbs up or thumbs down. Above the global chessboard of such moves hovers the sour, weary demon of uncertainty, and he cannot be driven off by all the exorcisms of the experts. A famous painter exhibits six perfectly black canvases. A joke, a challenge, or a valid idea? A refrigerator without a door, on bicycle wheels, and painted with stripes—is that acceptable? A chair pierced by three knives—is that art? But what do such questions mean when there are shows, when there are viewers and buyers, and critic-apologists, and in ten or twenty years the thing becomes petrified in art-history textbooks as a movement past and irretrievable? Uncertainty remains, however; hence works are not called by their names but, instead, given interpretational hedges. These are, we hear, quests, attempts, experiments. The future historian of twentieth-century art will state, with a smile, that the period produced practically nothing but proposed a great deal.

The artist, meanwhile, surrounded only by useful objects, exploits them. Everything serves a purpose—listening to music, shaving, moving from one place to another, grinding flour or baking bread. One can roll a millstone to a gallery, but the small degree of one's personal contribution to that creative act is sadly apparent. One must do something with the object, remove its function, so that what is left is perforce pure expression, the unalloyed aesthetic. That is how "machines for no purpose" come about. I, too, built them. Not as a trailblazer; as a child. The contemporary artist thus attempts to become a child at the heart of civilization, to recapture, in the child, lifesaving limits. For only a child does not know doubt, does not know of the flood of conventions—his game alone is serious. But does the artist find what he seeks in the child, safety from the bottomless pit of excessive freedom? He longs to return to the beginning of beginnings, where work was also play and also a creative act, where a deed was its own reward and needed no reason or goal outside itself. Yes, this was the state in which I made my pseudomachines. I built them because I needed them, and I needed to build them. A perfectly closed circle—like the ultimate circle of a faith that says it is All—but mine was natural because I was only twelve. I did all that I was able, pursued no real goals, and the only restrictions on me were imposed by nature and by my age. Unlike the artist, I did not try to be a child. What else could I have been?

The poor artist, seeking limits in the child, cannot fit himself in the child. True, it is a quiet, unconditional faith that pulls from a man the words *Credo quia absurdum est*. And true, there is nothing more absurd in our civilization, which is a pyramid of machines that serve purposes, than a machine that serves none. But the absurdity really lies in the fact that different paths lead to the same result. It is not good for a challah or river rock or furnace register to be mistaken for a work of art. It is not good when the photograph of a cross section of a mineral, or the slide of a stained tissue specimen, or a virus colony dusted with silver ions and seen through an electron microscope can be placed among abstract canvases and be their equal. Not that I dislike abstract paintings—not at all; there are excellent ones—yet even better work can be found among laboratory slides, or on a blackened strip of bark in a forest, where some white mold has embroidered its biological rhythm.

The misfortune of modern art is not that it is an artificial construct. Quite the contrary. Nature animate and inanimate is full of "abstract compositions." The microbiologist, geologist, and mathematician know them; they are present in the pseudomorphs of old dolerite, in the structures of amoebas, in the veins of leaves, in clouds, in the formations of eroded cliffs; and the two great creating-destroying master artists in this field are Entropy and Enthalpy. He who does not wish to compete with them (understanding, as few do, that in the end he will lose), and seeks safety in a return to the sweet prehistoric, hides in the child, in the primitive—to no avail, because the child and the Neanderthal acted earlier, and authentically.

But by what authority do I say all this? By none. You are free to disagree with me, particularly as I have no new prison to propose, no saving closure. And yes, I admit, alas, that I was a great trailblazer, and my classmates were, too, even in elementary school, when we stirred with a stick a puddle that had a drop of spilled gasoline in it, creating brief but beautiful color studies. We were great if snot-nosed primitivists, and my pseudopodia are to Calder's mobiles what Bosch is to the surrealists. And what compositions we made, even before that, out of a bowl of cream of wheat interspersed with spinach! Or, if you are interested in conceptual performance art, may I remind you—this time with pride—of the music box I urinated into? The twisted act of filling a mechanism of clockwork harmony with a bodily fluid of low regard—is this not the clash between the Newtonian idea (the clockwork notion of the heavenly spheres) and the principle of animal decay? And is not the juxtaposition of Ideal and Excrement truly avant-garde, the prophetic voice of catastrophic nihilism? At the tender age of four I discredited the lifeless determinism of music by an existential act, a blow struck for animal freedom, a slap in the face to centuries of conformity, a spontaneous creation, perfectly useless hence disinterested, pure . . .

One can go on and on. For all has turned out to be convention, language, too, the alphabet, the rules of grammar and syntax, and if the field of what is permissible widens enough, and if there can be an agreement of sorts about meanings assigned to objects, then absolutely anything can be expressed—with any sign, symbol, thing, picture. You will be able to place on exhibit severed fingers. Chairs that have, instead of a back, the rib cage and spine of a human skeleton and legs of human bone instead of wood. A giant onion, signifying the epistemology of cosmic matter: the many—and unending—layers of the knowledge of it, peeled off one by one, since there is no longer a monolithic Truth held by society, and no garbage dump anywhere that with the right lighting and frame does not make some clever, dark statement about civilization. Because a darkening cloud has taken the place of Truth, a blurring of information in which here and there individual works of art flicker with their own sad light, longing irrationally to be free of their freedom. But we have long digressed, our subject being not grown-up matters but a child. Let us return to him.

CHAPTER

7

LITTLE REMAINS FOR me to describe. Meanwhile, a host of objects in the house, and the streets I walked, which have not been mentioned, clamor for attention. What is it about the objects and cobblestones surrounding us in childhood that is so magical, so irreplaceable? Whence comes their demand that after the destruction of war and with them piled in rubbish heaps, I testify to their existence? Not many years after the idyllic time presented here, inanimate things were envied their permanence, for day by day people were taken from their midst, and suddenly the things were orphaned, the chairs, canes, and knickknacks abandoned and monstrously useless. As if objects were superior to the living, hardier than they, less vulnerable to the catastrophes of time. As if liberated from their owners, they had gained force and expression—consider the baby carriages and washbasins on the barricades, the eyeglasses there was no one to look through, the piles of letters stepped on. Although in the landscape of war they gained the power of eerie signs, I never held that against them. I believed in their innocence.

Untouched by fire and time is my affection for the old faience owl in my father's library; the lion and tiger, those heavy, beautiful creatures of blackened bronze; the chess set whose kings and pawns had Tatar faces, carved for my father by a fellow prisoner of war in a Russian camp in 1915; the two dog-clocks on my mother's dresser, showing the hour by the turns of their bulging eyes. I remember, in my parents' commonplace, very middle-class bedroom, a pane of a casement window that had a round hole with cracks in the glass running out toward the frame. I was told that a bullet did that during the battles of 1918. Deliberative child that I was, I looked for a mark in the ceiling, following the trajectory, but the surface there was smooth, unbroken. They had plastered the hole, they told me. But whether I couldn't believe that or didn't want to, in the quiet, ordinary apartment full of bourgeois affluence my eyes kept returning to the small, high pane. The hole apparently was not large enough to merit changing the pane. Did it disturb me, as Robinson Crusoe was disturbed by a footprint on the shore of his desert island? No, I did not see it as an omen of the cruelty to come—that cruelty would have been beyond my imagining in any case. The hole simply did not go with the sleepy harmony of the furniture. That trace was an astounding thing, like a detail taken from an impossibility that unexpectedly presents itself before you and calmly insists on its unquestionable, physical existence. Could it be that someone actually shot at the windows? At our apartment? And that I was born three years later?

But I must not exaggerate. The hole in the window always surprised me, perhaps even pained me as a sharp dissonance, but no more than that. It was no more remarkable than the drops of sap exuded by the frame of the same window. I loved to collect them on my finger, each drop slowly, because it took a few days for it to appear through the wood, through the varnish, a tear that was a little dry on the surface but inside fragrant, resinous, sticky. As if the wood were not reconciled to its fate, as if its unseen interior were still in the forest, stubbornly denying the reality of the plane, the nails, the varnish, and the two metal pieces that fastened the narrow strip of the blind to the frame.

So what exactly was it that formed the bond between the child walking those streets—always the same streets—and their pavement and walls? Beauty? I saw no beauty, did not know that the city could be different, that it could not go in folds of stone, could not be hilly, that streets like Copernicus and Sextus didn't have to soar upward, or the trams claw their way to the top and careen down. I did not see the Gothic architecture of Elizabeth Church or the eastern exoticism of the Armenian Cathedral. If I raised my head, it was to look at the metal hens turning on the chimneys.

It is amazing that I am at all able, straining against the current of time with my memory, to restore innocence to such words as Janow, Zniesienie, Piaski, Lackiego, to which the years 1941 and 1942 gave such evil meaning, when the streets from Bernstein's and past the theater, toward Sloneczna and beyond, one day were empty, silent, their windows open and curtains moving in the wind. The walls, courtyards, balconies—deserted, and in the distance appeared, then disappeared, the wooden fence of the ghetto. I saw the far, scattered buildings outside the city, then only rubble overgrown with grass.

In the thirties no one saw this coming. Though there was sometimes trouble. From the balcony of our apartment, crouching, I watched mounted police charge a crowd of demonstrators—it was during the funeral of Kozak. As rocks clattered on the metal shutters which the merchants used to try to save their windows, I saw one policeman in a shining helmet pulled off his horse. But this passed like a sudden storm, and when the janitors swept the broken glass off the sidewalk, peace returned, and nuns—my father's grateful patients—brought from their garden great armfuls of grafted lilacs, which we put under running water in the bathtub, and on the "Merry Lvov" station we listened to the comedians Toncio and Szczepiec and the funny monologues, with much throat-clearing from Mr. Stroncio, and I told my parents that I wouldn't go to gymnasium because you had to wear knickerbockers, which I hated because they tickled under the knee. We were like ants bustling in an anthill over which the heel of a boot is raised. Some saw its shadow, or thought they did, but everyone, the uneasy included, ran about their usual business

until the very last minute, ran with enthusiasm, devotion
—to secure, to appease, to tame the future. Adults and children, we were all made equal by the blessing of ignorance,
without which one cannot live.

We prepared ourselves. Every day we wore uniforms
to school, and once a week there was a military-training
lesson and we had to wear a different uniform, which was
a green linen tunic put on over the head like a Russian
gimnastyorka. Students pinned various badges on their
chest, Scout badges, sharpshooting medals. As for me, after
strewing a great number of cartridges on the firing range
by Highcastle, I received a gold sharpshooter's medal before I graduated—but didn't have long to glory in it. The
tunic was worn with the front smoothed out under a wide
belt. Some of us had elegant belts with double buckles and
lots of stitching. I got one like that; it even had a felt lining
and brass hooks for an officer's diagonal strap across the
chest, which of course I had no right to. For that tunic you
needed to be thin, like L., whose waist could be spanned
with two hands, and a big behind made the folds in back
flare like a tail, turning the uniform into a skirt. This tormented me.

The commander of our corps was Professor Starzewski,
a historian and reserve officer, but he kept himself above
us, that is, at a distance. On an everyday basis we were seen
to by several noncommissioned officers who came from
downtown, often carrying little packages that contained
military secrets—for example, vials that when you lifted the
cork, you got a whiff (harmless) of poison gas. They let us
smell phosgene, bromobenzyl, cyanide, chloroacetophe-
none, and various other invisible poisons with equally om-

inous names. We were also given gas masks during these exercises. I remember their unpleasant rubber-canvas smell and taste. It was hard to breathe in them; you gasped when you ran, but this was still just a game.

Once, on the playing field, they set off smoke bombs, and the sergeant threw a tear-gas grenade. The wind shifted, and the cloud enveloped the janitor, who emerged from it crying like a baby. The noncoms had a lot of trouble with us. We laughed behind their backs and made up names for them. We had our own rifles—in our microscopic gymnasium arsenal—mostly Lebels of 1889 make, I think. An archaic weapon, long and heavy, though repeating. The cartridges were fed one at a time into a slot below the firing chamber, the bolt being opened and closed countless times. There was a lot of drill and presenting of arms, but only very rarely did we get even blanks to fire—and that was outside the city, of course, somewhere in the Kaiserwald, to which we marched in a column.

The sights of our rifles were uncalibrated, but these weapons clearly were not meant for battle; we might just as well have drilled with wood carved in the shape of rifles. But complaining about the quality of our arms would probably have been considered high treason. When the weather was bad, we spent the two hours in class cleaning our rifles. It was an art in itself, a little Danaidean, a little Sisyphean, in the midst of enormous quantities of oakum and petroleum jelly. We also learned how to check our work—with a match whittled to a toothpick, which the sergeant delicately poked around the screws of the butt and between the stock and barrel. It was always possible to find some minuscule crevice that would dirty the tip of the wood, and then you had to start all over. But it didn't really anger us—as if we understood that such were the rules of the game, and that this was what the military was based on.

In the second year of lyceum we went to the firing range with real rifles, not Lebels. The mood was front-line. We had been prepared for this so long, and for the Mausers used in the army, but we were not allowed to touch them until the very last moment, and the rounds were distributed to us with great mystery and caution only at the concrete stands and only one apiece, such miserliness giving the rifle gigantic significance, making it a weapon whose power nothing could resist, a rare and accurate instrument such as few other armies in the world possessed. And the atmosphere intensified: the concrete stands of the firing range, the powerful kick of the weapon if you did not press the butt correctly into your shoulder. In comparison with the KB, what was the paltry .22 we had sometimes fired when we were in gymnasium! Even Julek D.'s repeater no longer impressed.

Amusing, that the whole purpose of a military rifle was something we—or at least I, but I think this applied to others, too—did not really think about. The targets, true, were not innocent circles but silhouettes, pale green, that wore helmets and had white blotches for faces; but this, too, was a conventional target. The point was to score, not to kill—there was no talk, somehow, of killing.

Not even when we had bayonet practice. Which I didn't like. Our weapon there was a long piece of wood in the rough shape of a rifle, and its jutting end was wrapped with rags, like a hard fist of cloth. The basic posture was grotesque—legs wide apart and knees bent. We dueled in pairs or sometimes with the sergeant, who was a master of the bayonet, or else we attacked enormous, lumbering dolls that looked a little like tailor's dummies. The sergeant showed us where to jab and how, and loved to talk about different kinds of bayonets, the Polish flat bayonet and the one with a square blade, and how after you shoved it in, you had to twist it to tangle the entrails. Then he showed us, but only theoretically, what you could do with an ordinary folding shovel, what a terrific tool it was; if you hit with it between the neck and collarbone and were lucky, you could take off a whole arm at the shoulder. But not to aim for the head, for God's sake; the head would probably have a helmet, and the shovel would only bounce off. We were also shown how to parry a bayonet thrust with such a shovel, and we threw grenades, that is, mock grenades. And then, again, long hours of cleaning our clumsy Lebels while it rained.

Only once did we go into the city with our rifles, an extraordinary circumstance. It was after the death of Marshal Pilsudski, in the evening. Why in the evening, I do not know. We marched in the present-arms position the whole time, our arms numb from the heavy Lebel pulled to the belt, and made a great circle through the city, through Mariacki Square, where not far from the Mickiewicz monument, invisible in the darkness then, stood a lonely pedestal, not large, with a stone bust bound with a black sash, under a floodlight. And we marched, tramping the pavement as hard as we could, to a mournful drumbeat that seemed to fill the city. The year was 1935.

During the three years of my military training, there was no mention made, not once, of the existence of tanks. They simply didn't matter. We studied every kind of gas and the names of the parts of guns, and regulations, and how sentries are posted, and ground tactics, and many other things. About a hundred hours a year of such instruction, three hundred in the upper classes, but it was—I see this now—as if they were preparing us for a war like the Franco-Prussian War of 1870. We did not belong to the army, were not even a small reserve, only the idea of one. Multiply us, with our anachronistic, worthless training, thousands, tens of thousands of times, and you have a sense of the tremendous labor undertaken by men in uniform—to no end. The defeat has overshadowed everything; and yet, looking back, I am still dismayed by that great waste.

My last summer vacation before graduation I spent at a training camp in Delatyn. It was like being in the army, on maneuvers. We lived eighteen men to a tent, near the high, steep bank of the Prut, with everything military: reveille, drills, field exercises, meals from a cauldron, tactics, and evening roll call. It was my first time away from home—no one to care for me but section leaders and noncoms. They let us know right off that we would be treated as adults, soldiers, and the captain warned against contact with the local female population because there was a lot of syphilis among the mountaineers.

I learned many things, among them the mechanism of power. When it was my turn to be orderly, I went in the morning to the quartermaster-sergeant to get our tent's allotment of marmalade. The sergeant sliced off a large portion of the raspberry substance for himself and handed me the rest. On my way back I understood what I was supposed to do, and in turn took my own cut.

Toward the end of the vacation there were big maneuvers in the presence of a Warsaw observer, a major. He seemed to us a towering general. To avoid the problems connected with carrying the folding shovel, which hit me in the back when I ran, I took advantage of the fact that only every other student received a shovel, and began to pretend that I had never been issued one. I hid mine (on the advice of a kindly section leader) in my straw mattress. I had to pay for it, but at least I got out of the drudgery of entrenching. I also solved the problem of my Lebel: listening to the civilian who sat within me, I cleaned the inside of its barrel to a silver shine, then plugged the muzzle with a small, inconspicuous cork so no dirt could get in during all the jumping and falling. Thus, when I cleaned the rifle, I needed to polish only the surface, and during inspection, at the right moment, I secretly removed the cork.

My colleague Miecio R. did not fare as well. In an intermission in the big maneuvers he was singled out for some reason by the major himself and ordered first to demonstrate the correct procedure for a gas alert. When the major shouted, "Gas attack!," Miecio turned pale, and before the sharp eyes of all the top brass he finally opened his metal canister, which instead of a mask contained apples and candy. He had hid his mask in his straw mattress. The consequences of this were to be dreadful, including a failing grade on his report card, but then the whole thing somehow was forgotten.

The maneuvers themselves I remember as a great deal of running about and shooting blanks. For which they woke us at four in the morning. I observed that at that hour in

July the world was incredibly lovely, and promised myself that in civilian life also I would enjoy the early morning. But this never happened. We did plenty of crawling and, not ever knowing where the enemy was, fired in all directions to be safe. Then our advance guard got lost, and we encountered a mountaineer woman, who began to follow us, then suddenly she jumped on our section leader's back and got his rifle. It turned out to be one of the corporals, fiendishly disguised to demonstrate to us the trickery of war.

We won, I think, though I'm not sure. A few more times they woke us in the middle of the night for an attack, and if our shoelaces weren't all tied right, back we had to go under the blankets and start again. One night we dressed and undressed something like four times at record speed. But what I remember most is that in the army you were always cleaning something—if not a weapon, then boots, if not boots, then the floor (there was no floor in the tents, so here cleaning revealed its completely symbolic nature).

This was the first time—on this vacation—that I saw poverty close up. The mountaineers were extremely poor: for five groszy or a hunk of bread you could get a heaping mess-tin of raspberries or strawberries, and they thought they were getting a bargain. Delatyn, not like Tatarow or Jaremcze, was off the beaten path for tourists.

For several days we worked in water, rebuilding a bridge that the swollen river had swept away. The sun turned me as dark as an African. An end finally came to our mock warfare, and all the rituals took place—tossing noncoms and lieutenants into the air, and those not liked, those who had given us a hard time, met with fists on their way down instead of open hands. I remember how we chased one of the lieutenants through the camp, a pig-faced blond who turned apoplectic red in the sun. He tried to restrain us with orders, but the bubble of authority and obedience had broken, and nothing could help him—up into the air he went.

The rifle improved my posture, and I even lost weight. On the last day there was a campfire with singing, fizzy lemonade, and doughnuts, and the next morning they put us on the train. On the way to Lvov, one of the instructors, an officer-cadet, sat next to me, told me he really liked me—more, admired me. Friendship from an officer, admiration no less (but for what?)—it staggered me. When it turned out that he liked my boots (I had two pair), I was happy to part with them—except I didn't know how to make the offer without offending him, given his high rank. Fortunately, the officer-cadet took care of this for me and, holding the boots by their back loops, disappeared. The train was just then pulling in under the enormous vault of the main station, where my anxious parents were waiting for me.

EPILOGUE

Nobody died when I was little. I heard of such things, yes—as one hears of meteors. Everyone knows they fall, but what does that have to do with us? While writing this book, between one rainy Zakopane day and another, I dreamed of my father. Not indistinct and of indeterminate age, as I see him when I am awake, but in a specific moment, alive. I saw his gray eyes behind his glasses, eyes not yet weary, and the trimmed mustache and small beard, and his hands with short fingernails—the always scrubbed hands of a doctor—and his gold ring grown thinner with wear. The folds of his vest, the coat pulled a little to the right by the weight of the laryngologist's mirror—and, behind him, the apartment, the wallpaper, the old tall stove with the white tiles and their network of tiny cracks, and a thousand other details I was unable to name when I woke. All this is inside me, an inaccessible host of memories, sequences of minutes, hours, days, weeks, years—and nothing can enter there except dream, whose movement I have no control over. Stryjski Park is in there somewhere, all in snow, and my father walking on a path between dark trees, his freezing hands in the pockets of his overcoat, while I, on skis for the first time, can hardly move my legs, imagining myself a king of infinite space. The clop of hoofs suddenly dulled on the wooden pavement of Marszalkowska in front of Jan Casimir University, and the long screech of a tram hitting the windows of the classroom as it turns around our playing field to begin the arduous climb to Highcastle. All the banisters I slid down at school; the checkered knickerbockers of my colleague Loza, the longest in the class; the green bumper cars at the Eastern Fair; all the chestnuts. The copper kettle for hot water on the kitchen stove; the acorns on the bedroom ceiling; the scrap iron at the flea market, through which I looked for treasures; and even my first bed, white, enclosed on the side with string netting. The ship that by some miracle sailed into a bottle through the narrow neck. The first legal cigarette, with a red cloth filter tip, a "Nile," which I smoked after graduation in June 1939.

And what avalanches descended on that world. How was

it they did not wipe it out completely, erasing every trace? And for whom exactly do the traces survive? For whom does memory preserve them, reluctant memory, opening its treasury only at night, in insensible sleep, to the blind dreamer? In the light of day memory is stubborn, tight-fisted, giving brief, cryptic answers which have to be laboriously deciphered, the gaps filled in with guesses; and when suddenly some fragment is pulled from memory by force or stealth—a blotch of color, the outline of someone's lips, a shadow, a sound—there is no explanation, only the vague but persistent conviction that it had to do with something important, fateful, but there is only emptiness, blank as a wall, and we can do nothing. Our thoughts are like underground tunnels that collapse. Although tight-fisted and indifferent, memory knows everything and can but will not help; it is contemptuous, locked in itself, ignoring the passage of time, independent of time. If it were indeed just a void with a few fading images flitting here and there—but no, it is definitely not that; there is evidence, dreams. And it keeps denying me admittance where I wish to go, letting me in only elsewhere, and never when I want. Stupid latched gate. Sovereign machine stupidly preoccupied with its function, its task: to record, preserve indelibly, permanently. But that is not true either. It will perish with me, fanatical guardian, miser tyrant, mocking, disobedient, stiff-necked, so invariable and yet so uncertain, uncaring and at the same time sensitive, like a lump of coal that bears the delicate impression of a leaf. How am I to understand memory? How come to terms with it? Neural nets, synapses, McCulloch loops? No, there is no explaining it in that wise, absurdly scientific way—it's useless, let memory remain as it is. Memory and I are a pair of horses eyeing each other distrustfully, pulling one wagon. So let us go, my inseparable, unknown companion, my enemy, my friend.